Four Birds

Birds

of Noah's Ark

Also by Robert Hudson

Kiss the Earth When You Pray: The Father Zosima Poems

The Christian Writer's Manual of Style

Companions for the Soul (with Shelley Townsend-Hudson)

Beyond Belief: What the Martyrs Said to God
  (Duane W. H. Arnold and Robert Hudson)

*The Monk's Record Player: Thomas Merton, Bob Dylan,
  and the Perilous Summer of 1966* (forthcoming)

Four Birds

of Noah's Ark

{ *a prayer book from
the time of* Shakespeare }

edited with an introduction by Robert Hudson

William B. Eerdmans Publishing Company
Grand Rapids, Michigan

WM. B. EERDMANS PUBLISHING CO.
2140 Oak Industrial Drive NE, Grand Rapids, Michigan 49505
www.eerdmans.com

Published 2017
Published in association with the literary agency of
Credo Communications, LLC, Grand Rapids, MI 49525
www.credocommunications.net
Printed in the United States of America

26 25 24 23 22 21 20 19 18 17   1 2 3 4 5 6 7 8 9 10

ISBN 978-0-8028-7481-8

Library of Congress Cataloging-in-Publication Data

Names: Dekker, Thomas, approximately 1572–1632, author. |
    Hudson, Bob, 1953– editor.
Title: Four birds of Noah's Ark : a prayer book from the time of Shakespeare /
    Thomas Dekker ; edited with an introduction by Robert Hudson.
Description: Grand Rapids : Eerdmans Publishing Co., 2017. |
    Includes bibliographical references.
Identifiers: LCCN 2017020667 | ISBN 9780802874818 (pbk. : alk. paper)
Subjects: LCSH: Prayers. | Birds—Miscellanea.
Classification: LCC BV245 .D455 2017 | DDC 242/.8—dc23
    LC record available at https://lccn.loc.gov/2017020667

Contents

INTRODUCTION "Thomas Dekker and His Four Birds" 1
  Robert Hudson

PROLOGUE "To the Reader" 19
  Thomas Dekker

PART ONE: THE DOVE 23

  *Prayers of Blessing for the Poor, the Humble,
  and All Those Who Labor in the Cities and Fields*

PART TWO: THE EAGLE 61

  *Prayers of Blessing for the Nation
  and All Those Entrusted with Authority*

PART THREE: THE PELICAN 97

  *Prayers of Supplication to Christ
  to Help Us Overcome the Seven Deadly Sins*

PART FOUR: THE PHOENIX 123

  *Prayers of Thanksgiving for the Benefits We
  Receive in the Death and Resurrection of Christ*

v

PART FIVE: FEATHERS   143
   *Short, Pithy Meditations to
   Accompany the Prayers in This Book*

Listing of Prayers by Part Title   155

Notes   159

Bibliography   165

Acknowledgments   167

Thomas Dekker and His Four Birds

Just when we think we've unearthed all the great Christian classics of the past, new ones emerge to surprise and enchant us. The book you hold in your hands is just such a classic. It is an Elizabethan playwright's own volume of intimate prayers—poetic, moving, accessible, and timeless—as powerful today as they were four hundred years ago. While thousands of Londoners fled the Black Death that ravaged the city in 1608, this book's author remained and, amid the tragedy around him, penned these fervent prayers in honor of the ordinary working people for whom he had such a deep and enduring affection. Had Shakespeare written prayers, they would certainly not have been any more beautiful than the ones in this volume: *Four Birds of Noah's Ark*.

The founding editor of the Everyman's Library series of classics, Ernest Rhys, once pronounced *Four Birds of Noah's Ark* to be "a very remarkable book of prayers . . . [of] profound eloquence and power of devotional expression,"[1] and no less a poet than Algernon Swinburne described the book as "a work of genius so curious and so delightful that the most fanatical of atheists or agnostics, the hardest and the driest of philosophers, might be moved and fascinated by the exquisite simplicity of its beauty."[2]

As a writer, editor, and poet, I have read and reread these

prayers for more than thirty years, and their beauty and power have yet to grow stale. I seem to find myself in nearly every corner of every prayer. I identify with the child going to school, with the apprentice learning his craft, with the parent raising a family, and with the woman on her sick bed. I glean personal comfort and hope from the prayers. My wish is that you, the reader, will find yourself in every corner of these prayers as well.

Who Was Thomas Dekker?

Despite the graceful piety of these prayers, their author, Thomas Dekker, was not an unusually pious man. He was not a minister nor a Bible scholar nor a theologian, nor was he in the forefront of the religious controversies of his time—of which there were many. He was not a spiritual writer, nor did any of his contemporaries so much as hint that he was particularly religious. Playwright Ben Jonson went so far as to call Dekker a "rogue."[3]

Instead, Dekker wrote lively, often rollicking plays for the popular theater. He collaborated with many of the well-known playwrights of the time, possibly even Shakespeare,[4] and ended up feuding with some, notably Jonson. Dekker also wrote prose that some later critics have described as journalistic hackwork, while others have praised him for being the "Charles Dickens of the Elizabethan age."[5] Like Dickens, he was an acute observer of all classes, taking special pleasure in describing London's lowlife, its villains and charlatans, and satirizing the city's foppish young-men-about-town—two species of humanity Dekker regularly encountered.

The times Thomas Dekker lived in were chaotic. When he was still a child, the Parliament of England made it a crime punishable by death to convert anyone to Catholicism, and so began the great wave of Catholic martyrs under Queen Elizabeth I. The English fleet defeated the Spanish Armada when Dekker was only sixteen, and he likely served in the military shortly after that. In his lifetime he survived four major London plagues. Elizabeth died and James ascended to the throne when Dekker was thirty-one, and when he was thirty-nine, in 1611, the King James Bible was published.

Apart from his reputation as a London bohemian and the large number of plays he wrote and collaborated on, scholars know few details about Dekker's life. Apart from his writings, our main source is the diary of one of London's most important theater moguls, Philip Henslowe, and his references to Dekker in the late 1590s are all financial: how much Dekker was paid for certain scripts and how much was paid in 1599 to spring Dekker from his first visit to debtors' prison. Although Dekker wrote many of the most popular plays of the era, money was tight. Living as a playwright in Elizabethan London was not easy, and unlike Shakespeare, Dekker was neither an actor nor a managing partner in a theater company. Prose writing, to which Dekker turned more often in the early 1600s, after leaving Henslowe's company, was generally more lucrative.

In 1612, Dekker found himself in debtors' prison—for the third time in his life—where he would remain for seven years. In one of his plays he slyly refers to prison as the "university" where "men pay more dear . . . for their wit than anywhere."[6] He puts this idea in more pathetic terms in his "Prayer for One in Jail": "Let this imprisonment, O Lord, always be to me a book in which I may read, first, the knowledge of you." His hair is said to have turned completely white during this third imprisonment. Still, after his release, he lived for another thirteen productive years.

Prison was the only "university" that Dekker attended, though he seems to have taken full advantage of his grammar school education. He learned enough Latin to be able to translate the "Short and Pithy Sentences," which serve as the concluding "Feathers" section of *Four Birds*. Judging from the many literary allusions in his plays, he was an avid reader and spoke French and Dutch fluently enough for his stage characters to speak them occasionally as well.

As a supplement to his education, Dekker found his richest material in the London of his time—its locales, its urban rhythms, its argot, its prisons, and its eccentrics. He was fully aware of London's place in the world, for, as he referred to it in "A Prayer for the City," London was "the greatest city . . . now upon earth . . . may [it] outshine all the cities of the world in goodness as it does in greatness." He was the first English writer to make London a major literary theme.

Though his work is considered uneven, especially compared to that of such contemporaries as Jonson and Shakespeare, Dekker was one of the most prolific playwrights of the age. One contemporary referred to his "right happy and copious industry."[7] No one knows exactly how many plays he wrote because much of his work is lost. Twenty of his plays found their way into print, but of his other plays, we know that far more have vanished than have been preserved.

His most frequent work was as a collaborator. He shared bylines on scores of scripts and undoubtedly contributed to many more for which he received no credit. He wrote poetry and polemics, and his prose works include numerous pamphlets and tracts—the journalism of the time—on such popular topics as the Gunpowder Plot, pickpockets, London's armor manufacturers, and the Black Death. Aside from his most famous play, *The Shoemaker's Holiday*, a true masterpiece that is still performed today, Dekker is best remembered—and remembered appreciatively—for his rich portrayals of day-to-day life in the London of Shakespeare's time.

From Dekker's writing we can surmise that he was an irrepressible optimist, due no doubt to his gregarious but determined personality and his tireless creativity. He had a sprightly sense of humor, a slashing wit, and a strong work ethic combined with a somewhat devil-may-care approach to business.

That he was a Christian is certain. One writer says slyly of Dekker that if he was "not over-particular in his manner of life, [he] had at least a marvelous facility in repentance."[8] Judging from his prayers, we sense that his faith arose from personal conviction and a clear understanding of the basics of Christian belief. Although *Four Birds* is the only book of devotion he wrote, there is no evidence to suggest that his religious feelings were anything but sincere. In most of his other writings, even in his most biting satires, Dekker's sensibilities lean heavily toward the moralistic, the sentimental, and the traditional.

The Plague Years

When London's public theaters closed in 1608 and 1609 due to an outbreak of plague, playwrights had to find other means of support. Although this bout of the Black Death was not as devastating as the one in 1603, the situation was dire.[9] Londoners prepared for the worst. Shakespeare returned to Stratford to escape the pestilence and to tend to his aging mother, who died later that year. He also became a business partner in the King's Men acting company and their upscale indoor theater, Blackfriars, for which he began writing his late romances. Ben Jonson and other playwrights spent their time creating masques, highly stylized stage spectacles, for the court. Though the London theaters might be closed, the nobility still insisted on their private entertainments.

Dekker, who much preferred popular audiences to the court, returned to prose. Along with three other works, he wrote his *Four Birds of Noah's Ark* at this time, which gives his "Prayer to Withhold the Pestilence" a special resonance: "Withhold the invader's arm," he prays, "who shoots darts of pestilence so thickly among us that we descend into the merciless grave in heaps." And he adds, "The living whom [Death] spares are not able to bury the carcasses as fast as he destroys them." Powerful words and images. Unlike most of his contemporaries, Dekker refused to avert his eyes from the daily tragedies that London's working folk experienced in plague time.

Scholars suggest that *Four Birds of Noah's Ark* was a bit of religious hackwork, written for wealthy patrons as a way of cashing in on the anxieties of the time. Throughout the centuries, publishers have known that during periods of economic and social instability, people seek out religious books for comfort, even while other types of books falter. Dekker was certainly aware of this—he was a professional writer, after all—but the fact that his book speaks to us so powerfully after so many centuries is a testimony to its sincerity and conviction. Scholar and biographer Mary Hunt summarized it well: "The charm [of *Four Birds*] lies in the man himself, in his profoundly religious nature, in the temperament of an artist as sensitive to the beauty of holiness as to other forms of beauty."[10]

Four Birds of Noah's Ark was printed in London in 1609, and sold, as the title page says, "at the shop Nathaniel Butter near St. Austin's Gate." Butter is now chiefly remembered as the printer of the pirated first quarto edition of Shakespeare's *King Lear* in 1608. Dekker's book of prayers was not a bestseller by any means, since Butter continued to list that edition in his catalogs for the next eight years. Since the plague had abated somewhat by the time the book actually appeared, much of the prayers' urgency had dwindled. Londoners were ready to return to the theater. No second printing appeared.

Of the other three nondramatic works that Dekker wrote during his break from playwriting, the most famous is *The Gull's Hornbook*, which satirizes the up-and-coming young gallants of London, whose main ambitions were to be noticed and to move up in society. In the comic guise of what we would now call an advice book, Dekker mocks these youths by describing their worst faults taken to extremes. In Chapter 6, "How a Gallant Should Behave Himself in a Playhouse," Dekker describes the custom of well-to-do audience members paying to sit on the stage during performances. Dekker recommends this to the young gallants so they can make themselves a nuisance, disrupting entrances and exits, playing cards when bored, talking loudly, and hooting at the actors for no particular reason. And "if you know not the author, you may rail against him and . . . enforce the author to know you."[11] Dekker himself must have suffered his share of abuse from the spoiled young toughs sitting on the stage during his own plays.

The tone of *The Gull's Hornbook* is satirical, in sharp contrast to the measured piety of *Four Birds*. And yet, one can't help but wonder if a little satire hasn't crept into the prayers here and there, as when Dekker places in the lawyer's mouth a prayer to be given neither poverty nor wealth, but "only . . . so much as may maintain my life." As someone who had spent time in prison and probably had a low view of lawyers, it may well have been a not-so-gentle jibe.

Four Birds of Noah's Ark

So, what makes *Four Birds of Noah's Ark* worthy of our attention four hundred years later? I believe that *Four Birds* possesses two fundamental traits that more than justify our close attention in the twenty-first century, that make these prayers masterpieces of English literature: empathy and imagination.

Nowhere else in Elizabethan or Jacobean literature do we find such heartfelt portraits of ordinary people as in Dekker's writing, especially *Four Birds of Noah's Ark*. Here we have prayers of a miner working in a mine, a sailor on the verge of perishing at sea and then surviving, a woman about to give birth and the midwife who attends her, a lawyer praying that God will keep him from being tempted to defraud others, and a sick woman facing mortality. With his strong imagination, Dekker envisions how a child shuffling off to school might pray and how Queen Elizabeth—with an entirely different set of concerns—would have addressed her God, formally, even imperially. These prayers are an inventive cross-section of society. As much as Shakespeare reveled in the language and foibles of the common people, he portrayed them as farcical characters as often as not. Dekker had a genuine affection for the ordinary folk who crowded the dirty London streets.

With empathy and imagination, an artist can't help but be aware of the spiritual reality in the world all around. Those traits are found in the most popular Christian writers, especially those who, like Dekker, were not religious professionals—writers like Bunyan, Tolstoy, Chesterton, C. S. Lewis, Walker Percy, Eudora Welty, and Flannery O'Connor, writers with brilliant insights into human character and the creative gift to be able to convey those insights to others.

Dekker's rich imagination led him to divide his book into four highly inventive categories, with each of the four birds representing a different kind of prayer. The Dove, being the most humble bird of all, represents the prayers of everyday working people, while the Eagle, being the most regal of birds, represents the prayers of the nobility and the leaders of the nation. The next two birds each represent Christ. In legend, the Pelican is said to feed its young with its own blood, which for Dekker becomes a symbol of Christ's sacrifice on the cross. Finally, the famous Phoenix (like Fawkes in the Harry Potter books), which dies in a fiery blaze and rises again from its own ashes, represents Christ's resurrection. In this way, Dekker manages to paint a sympathetic portrait of the entire world while outlining the fundamentals of Christian faith at the same time.

In light of the vast number of biblical allusions he makes, Dekker had more than a passing knowledge of the Bible. Mary Hunt wrote, "Much of Dekker's purity and clarity of phrase, at his best, sprang from his intimate knowledge of the Bible; in his prayers, biblical quotations are so interwoven with his own words as to appear a part of the very texture."[12] Nevertheless, he often appears to be quoting from memory, since many of his quotations don't precisely match either of the popular Bible versions of his time: the Great Bible of Miles Coverdale and the Geneva Bible. (Dekker, of course, wrote *Four Birds* three years before the publication of the King James Version.) His biblical quotations, like many of Shakespeare's, were filtered through the Anglican liturgy, the Book of Common Prayer.[13]

Dekker's language is surprisingly modern. His writing lacks the elaborate verbal flourishes common at the time. Many earlier Elizabethan writers were practitioners of a popular style called *euphuism*, which originated with poet John Lyly and which Shakespeare satirized in his play *Love's Labour's Lost* (c. 1598). Thomas Dekker wrote an unusually direct and unornamented prose. The only exception is the prayer he puts in the mouth of Queen Elizabeth, which is something of an outlier in this collection. Dekker wrote it in 1597, a decade before the other prayers, and it was composed when the highly convoluted, euphuistic style was at its most fashionable. Swinburne derided this particular prayer as "bloated bombast and flatulent pedantry."[14]

In most cases, Dekker is careful to write so as to make the depth of religious feeling his primary focus rather than trying to impress the reader with verbal fireworks. While these prayers are eloquent and measured, they are always heartfelt and direct. To that extent, Dekker's language is more like our own than Shakespeare's is.

As a dramatist, Dekker was unusually sensitive to voice, despite the fact that he was not an actor himself. The prayers of the common people in the Dove section of *Four Birds* are quite different in style, tone, and vocabulary from those in the Eagle section, which includes the prayers of the king and queen, their court, the nation's clergy, judges, lawyers, and so on. This makes an oral reading of these prayers almost like a dramatic recitation. One can picture each of these character "types" walking onto the stage to pray their set piece aloud before they exit and the next character walks on.

Also, a surprisingly democratic instinct runs through these prayers, which can be seen in Dekker's uncommon empathy for working people, the miners and the midwives, the sailors and soldiers. His prayers for the nobility are more formal, partake of less vivid imagery, urge humility upon them, and in many cases even direct the focus back to the necessity of treating the common folk with kindness. In the prayers for the clergy and the judges, for instance, his concern is that they be fair and tend to the needs of the poor.

Take, for example, his "Prayer for the Nobility," in which he says, "Since every good person, O Lord, is noble in your sight, make every person who is noble among us also to be good." From his plays, we gather that Dekker was not a fan of the king's court, but to say such a thing in 1608—that all people, of whatever class, are noble in God's eyes if only they are good—was, if not a revolutionary statement, then at least verging on being a provocative one. And to suggest that the nobles were no more virtuous by nature than the common people was equally astonishing.

Dekker is also more than just a good presenter of character. He is also able to move seamlessly into the realm of lay theology. In the third and fourth sections of *Four Birds*, he provides what are almost sermons on the fundamentals of the Christian faith, covering in detail the seven deadly sins and the seven benefits derived from Christ's death and resurrection. While many clerics in Dekker's England wrote entire books on those subjects, it would be hard to find any that are as concise, accessible, and lay-oriented as Dekker's. With his avoidance of academic terminology, he anticipates the popular theology of later centuries. Those sections read like *Mere Christianity* had it been written by Shakespeare.

For these reasons, Dekker still speaks to our spiritual condition today. *Four Birds* is a compelling artistic and spiritual masterpiece. As Mary Hunt says, "As a work of art, [Dekker's] prayer-book is almost flawless."[15]

Despite this, *Four Birds of Noah's Ark* is largely ignored by modern scholars. Stanley Wells never mentions it in his chapter on Dekker in his superb study *Shakespeare & Co.* R. B. McKerrow, in the introduction to his edition of *The Gull's Hornbook*, never mentions Dekker's book of prayers by name but manages to dismiss it as being "of less interest . . . of a religious turn."[16] Other than some facsimile reprints of Victorian compendiums of Dekker's writings, the most recent edition of *Four Birds* is F. P. Wilson's, published in 1924. In the fifty years before Wilson's volume, Dekker's works experienced a considerable revival, but it faded quickly after the First World War.

Although recent critics may have passed Dekker over, ordinary people have not. He is still quoted. Though you may be unaware of it, you are probably already familiar with bits of Dekker's writing. Not only is the common phrase "the merry month of May" credited to him,[17] but the Beatles—yes, the pop group—set one of his poems to music. If you know their *Abbey Road* album, then you have heard their memorable setting of one of Dekker's most famous poems, "Golden Slumbers," the first stanza of which is:

> *Golden slumbers kiss your eyes,*
> *Smiles awake you when you rise;*
> *Sleep, pretty wantons, do not cry,*
> *And I will sing a lullaby.*[18]

Paul McCartney replaced "pretty wantons" with "little darling," as a way of not only modernizing the language but addressing the song to Heather Louise, his wife Linda's daughter from a previous marriage. At the time of the recording of *Abbey Road*, the girl was six years old, and she was Paul's first exposure to parenthood.

The Dekker-McCartney connection is unexpected, but more surprising is the link between Dekker and C. S. Lewis.

Dekker was the kind of man whom the Inklings would have relished inviting to an evening at the Eagle and Child—and what intriguing questions Lewis in particular would have asked him! I have no doubt that the first question out of Lewis's mouth would have been, "Tell me, how did *Four Birds* come about?"

As a scholar of English literature, Lewis was familiar with Dekker's writings and occasionally quoted from them in his letters and essays.[19] In his *Studies in Medieval and Renaissance Literature*, Lewis asserts that the line "All life is but a wandering to find home" from Dekker's play *The Witch of Edmonton* is more than a "pious metaphor" and should be interpreted as an "exposition of medieval Christian doctrine."[20] Lewis argues that the worldview of Dekker's writing, and that of other medieval and Renaissance writers, was essentially Christian and best understood by those conversant with their Christian context.

That Lewis should use Dekker as an example is only natural. Lewis's own English tutor at Oxford, Frank Percy Wilson (1889-1963), was a leading Dekker scholar and was preparing an edition of *Four Birds of Noah's Ark* at the time Lewis studied with him. One wonders what Lewis, who was not yet a professing Christian, thought of Dekker's collection of ardent prayers. (It is Wilson's 1924 edition on which this new edition is largely based.) Wilson was also a general editor of the monumental Oxford History of English Literature Series and invited Lewis to write the volume *English Literature in the Sixteenth Century, Excluding Drama* (1954).

For his part, Dekker would have enjoyed his evening with the Inklings, though their smoking would have bothered him; he speaks disparagingly of tobacco in several of his plays. He also might have found them a bit tame, a little too bookish and provincial for his taste. Most of them did not live in London, after all, but in distant, bucolic Oxford. Still, Dekker certainly spent many evenings in pubs, hashing over politics, the theater, books, current events, and religion with friends. One need only look at the many references to such occasions in his plays. As the gregarious Simon Eyre, the hero of Dekker's *Shoemaker's Holiday*, said, "Let wine be plentiful as beer, and beer as water."[21]

Roustabout and man-about-town though he may have been, in the end Dekker was the kind of feisty uncle who, when he woke up on Sunday morning, was alert to the church bells ringing from the next block. And on those mornings when he did manage to drag himself up the street in time for services, he could sincerely pray: "Whether I sleep or wake, give your angels charge over me, that at whatever hour you call me, I may, like a faithful soldier, be found ready to encounter Death and to follow the Lamb wherever he goes. Amen."

Whatever his faults, he knew that all of life was indeed a "wandering to find home."

So, what are we to make of Thomas Dekker's "roguery"?

The rich body of Christian literature in English is filled with larger-than-life saints: valiant martyrs like Thomas More, William Tyndale, and Robert Southwell; persecuted dissenters like John Bunyan and George Fox; epic geniuses like John Milton and William Blake; and a host of brilliant poet-divines like John Donne, Thomas Traherne, George Herbert, and Gerard Manley Hopkins.

Even if Dekker was as roguish as Jonson claimed, which

is doubtful, I would argue that Christian literature is more than ready to add an amiable rascal or two to its ranks. Every family enjoys its slightly crazy but lovable uncle who comes to family reunions and causes a stir. In Dekker's time, even the most staunchly conservative were more likely to attend a performance of his riotous *Shoemaker's Holiday* than to read, say, Richard Hooker's *Of the Laws of Ecclesiastical Polity* (1597). As influential as Hooker's book was, it has never been accused of being fun. Dekker's rumored roguery humanizes him and, in an odd way, humanizes his readers. In this book we find an ordinary man who was an extraordinary writer, and at the same time, we find ourselves.

A Note on the Text

Dekker's English is that of Shakespeare and the King James Bible, both of which were major influences on modern English, but like them, Dekker is not always easy to read. A certain amount of modernization is necessary. Although I have tried to stay true to Dekker's original, I also want this volume to be a satisfying experience for contemporary readers. I have modernized the spelling, syntax, and grammar when needed, changing, for instance, the *thees* and *thous* to *yous*. When the vocabulary seemed obscure or likely to be misread (many words have changed meanings), I replaced Jacobean words with modern ones as close to Dekker's meaning as possible. A number of discreet cuts were made when the language became too repetitive or too full of brimstone and damnation. Some of the titles were modified for clarity or devotional purposes, and I have changed Dekker's gender-specific language to gender-neutral when it was clear that the male references refer to both men and women.

The biggest challenge was "A Prayer Made by the Virtuous and Renowned Queen Elizabeth of Happy Memory." The imagined formal language of the queen, the inscrutable punctuation, and her use of the first-person plural in referring to herself (because of her identification with the entire realm) were so convoluted—euphuistic—as to be incomprehensible. I have had to paraphrase portions of it and eliminate others, while attempting to adhere to the high-mindedness of the original.

The most obvious departure is that I have broken these prayers into short lines, not so much to make them look like poetry—though Dekker was a fine poet—as to group ideas together and to encourage the reader to read slowly and meditatively. In this I have taken a cue from both the Book of Common Prayer and Lancelot Andrewes's posthumously published *Private Devotions*, the latter being written around the same time as Dekker's *Four Birds*. Andrewes was one of the group of scholars who translated the King James Bible. Both the Book of Common Prayer and *Private Devotions* set their prayers in broken lines.

I have provided a few annotations where illumination seemed helpful. Dekker uses biblical quotations and echoes biblical phrases in nearly every line, but I have only annotated the sources when he attributes such quotes to specific books or characters, and I have placed such phrases in quotation marks.

Dekker wrote elaborate dedications to the patrons from whom he was hoping to receive money. While historically interesting, these dedications are conventional and often uncomfortably fulsome. Dekker was not above a little collection-plate passing as these prayers circulated among his patrons. Since these dedicatory letters are of lesser value, I have eliminated them from this edition.

If you are looking for a verbatim transcription of Dekker's original, with its antiquated spelling and archaic constructions, I recommend that you search for a copy of F. P. Wilson's 1924 edition, which can still be found online relatively cheaply.

Bible Readings

Finally, each prayer begins with a reference to a Bible passage in square brackets. These are not in Dekker's original but are provided for those readers who would like to use the prayers devotionally in combination with Bible reading. These prayers are, after all, meant to be prayed and reflected upon as part of one's personal time of meditation and worship. I recommend reading them out loud as a way of drawing out their meaning. May they bless each reader richly in their own way.

While Dekker himself quotes from both the Great Bible of Miles Coverdale (1540) and the Geneva Bible (1599), those Bibles are relatively hard to find today, and their language is often confusing. I recommend that you use the King James Bible instead. It's not only the most popular Bible in English, but its language is the closest to Dekker's own.

ROBERT HUDSON

FOUR
BIRDS
of NOAh's Ark

To the Reader

Reader, to comfort you I have sent four birds from Noah's ark, with four different messages, and I have changed the notes of those birds' voices into prayers of different music—but all full of sweetness.

Under the wings of the *Dove* I have put prayers fitting the nature of the Dove, which is to say, simple prayers or such as are appropriate to the mouths of the young and the common people, and for such blessings as they most have need of.

The *Eagle* soars higher and in its beak bears up to heaven supplications in behalf of kings and rulers.

The *Pelican* carries the image of our Redeemer on the cross, who shed his blood to nourish us—he being the true Pelican. With a drop of that blood I have written prayers against all those deadly and capital sins, to wash out the foulness for which our Savior suffered that ignominious death.[1]

And lastly, in the spiced nest of the *Phoenix*, in which bird Christ is also figured in his rising again, you will find a book written full of thanks and wishes: of thanks for those benefits that we gain by Christ's death and resurrection; of wishes that he would in different gifts bestow those blessings upon us.

Nothing that is set down here is tedious, because I took care to keep you, the reader, in mind. Nothing is repetitious, so that you might take delight in these prayers. If you are young, here is pleasure for you; if old, here is comfort. If you are poor, here are riches; if you have enough, here is more.

Use the medicine well, and live well.

Run this race truly, and die well.

That is the goal: win that, win heaven.

What Prayer Is

Prayer is the language in which we talk to God, for when we read the Book, God speaks to us, but when we pray, we speak to him. It is, therefore, a dialogue between God and us.

It is that ladder that Jacob saw ascending up to the clouds, for on those stairs we climb up to heaven.

It is the compass by which we sail there.

It is the badge by which a Christian is known as serving God.

It is our best friend who speaks to God on our behalf.

It is the only eloquence that persuades God.

It is the only music that charms God's anger to sleep.

It is our peacemaker in the wars between God and us.

It is the sword of defense in the combat between us and the devil.

It is the ship in which, if our souls sail not, we perish.

It is the anchorage at which we lie safe in the storms of Death.

It is the balm that cures the wounds of poverty, oppression, imprisonment, banishment, despair, cares, sorrows, and all calamities that hang like diseases upon our life.

Such is prayer. Such armor must we put on if we mean to win heaven.

THOMAS DEKKER

THE DOVE

*Prayers of Blessing for the Poor, the Humble,
and All Those Who Labor in the Cities and Fields*

....

THE EAGLE

*Prayers of Blessing for the Nation
and All Those Entrusted with Authority*

....

THE PELICAN

*Prayers of Supplication to Christ
to Help Us Overcome the Seven Deadly Sins*

....

THE PHOENIX

*Prayers of Thanksgiving for the Benefits We Receive
in the Death and Resurrection of Christ*

....

FEATHERS

*Short, Pithy Meditations to Accompany
the Prayers in This Book*

....

PART ONE

The DOVE

Prayers of Blessing for the Poor, the Humble,

and All Those Who Labor in the Cities and Fields

To the Reader

The Dove was the first bird that being sent out of Noah's ark brought comfort to Noah. So prayer being sent out of the ark of our bodies is the only and first bringer of comfort to us from heaven.

The Dove went out twice before it could find an olive branch (which was the sign of peace). So our prayers must fly up again and again and never stop beating at the doors of heaven until they fetch from there the olive branch of God's mercy as a symbol that we are at peace with our Lord and that our sins have been pardoned.

The Dove no sooner brought that bough of good tidings into the ark than the universal flood receded and sank into the bowels of the deep. So no sooner do our hearty prayers pierce the bosom of the Lord Almighty than the waters of divine indignation shrink away, melting like hills of snow to nothing; and the universal deluge of sin that flows forty days and nights together (which is to say, every hour of all our lifetime), to drown both soul and body, is driven back and ebbs into the bottomless gulf of hell.

The Dove is said to be without gall. Our prayers must be without bitterness and not to the detriment of our neighbor (for such prayers are curses), lest we pull down vengeance on our heads.

Such was the Dove that Noah sent out of the ark. With such wings let our prayers carry our messages up to heaven.

A Prayer for a Child Going to School

[Matthew 19:13-15]

O God, who is the fountain of all wisdom[1]
    and the founder of all learning,
        breathe into my soul the spirit of understanding
    so that in my childhood I may learn and,
    as I grow further in years, practice
    only the study of you and your laws.
Feed me, O Lord, as babes are fed, with the milk
    of your holy Word so that I may grow strong
    in setting forth your praises.
        Make me, O Jesus, Son of God, one of those
    of whom you say: "Suffer the little children
    to come unto me, and forbid them not."[2]
    And as you have promised that your wonders
    should be sounded forth by the tongues
    of infants and sucking babes, so pour into my lips
    the waters of the well of life, so that whatever
    I learn may be to proclaim your glory.
Polish my mind, O God, that it may shine bright
    in goodness and that I may not defile nor deface
    this temple of my body by corrupted manners
    or lewd speech but may season my tongue
    so that all the lessons I learn may seem
    to have been taught to me in your own school
Be my Schoolmaster to instruct me,
    that I may repeat the rules of true wisdom.
Make me obedient to my parents,
    dutiful to my teachers,
    loving to my schoolfellows,
    humble to my superiors,
    full of reverence toward the elderly,

proud toward no one—
    so that I may win the love of all.
Bless me, O Lord, this day;
    guide my feet,
    direct my mind,
    sanctify my studies,
    govern all my actions,
    preserve my body in health,
    my soul from uncleanness.
Grant this, O my God, for your Son's sake, Jesus Christ;
    and if it be your pleasure to cut me off
    before night, so that this flower of my youth
    shall fade in all the beauty of it,
    yet make me, O my gracious Shepherd,
    one of your lambs, to whom you will say,
    "Come, blessed";[3] and clothe me
    in a white robe of righteousness,
    so that I may be one of those singers
    who will cry to you, "Alleluia."[4] Amen.

A Prayer for a Farmer

[2 Timothy 2:6]

The earth, O Lord, is your garden in which
 you have appointed me to be a laborer.
 Of that stuff in which I daily dig and delve
 I am made; so that in trimming the earth,
 I do but dress myself.
Although Paul plants and Apollos waters,[5]
 no herb or flower can come up or tree prosper
 unless your hand prepares the soil.
 Therefore, send forth a wholesome breath
 from your nostrils upon those fruits of the earth
 that, out of the bounty of your love,
 you have bestowed upon me, your servant.
Let not the leaf of my labor wither,
 but prosper it till it grows up
 like a cedar on the heights of Lebanon,
 or like a tree planted by the waterside,[6]
 bringing forth fruit in due season.
 Restrain, O my God, the northern wind,
 that it beat not down the farmer's hopes,
 but that the sickle may in due time
 send a ripe and plentiful harvest.
Strike not the ox at the plow with death
 nor the horse in the pasture with disease,
 though I confess that my sins deserve to have
 the plagues of Egypt fall on me and my cattle.
 But the wings of your mercy, O gracious God,
 spread farther than those of your justice.
 Shed therefore those comfortable beams
 upon me, a creeping worm upon the earth.
 And not only do I beg these worldly

and fading blessings at your hand,
but those rather that are heavenly
and that last forever.
Pour your abundant grace on my soul,
that it may be fruitful in good works
and always bring forth seeds of holiness.
Open my heart, that it may not be barren
of understanding you.
Clear my eyes, that they may behold the face
of ignorance and loathe her,
and that they may look upon the beauty
of your sacred wisdom and be enamored by it.
For these, and whatever else you think fit
for the health of my body or happiness of my soul,
I most humbly beseech you in the name
of your blessed Son, Jesus Christ.

A Prayer for an Apprentice Going to Work

[I Timothy 5:18]

O Builder of this world! whose workmanship
    is seen to be excellent even in the frames
    of the least and basest creatures that you
    have set together—cast a gracious eye upon me,
    and lend me your directing hand so that
    the labors I undertake this day may prosper.
Let me not, O God, go about my business
      with "eye service";[7]
    but since you have ordained that, like poor Joseph,
    I must enter into the state of an apprentice,
    so humble my mind that I may perform
    with cheerful willingness whatever my teacher
    commends me and that all his commendations
    may be agreeable to the serving of you.
Bestow upon me your grace,
    that I may deal uprightly with all humankind
    and that I may show myself to the one
    who is set over me, ruling as I would desire
    to have others behave themselves to me.
Take away from the one who is my teacher all thought
    of cruelty, so that like the children of Israel
    under subjection to Pharaoh's servants,
    I may not be set a task above my strength;
    or if I be, stretch out my sinews, O God,
    that I may with unwearied limbs accomplish it.
Fill my veins with blood so that I may go through
    the hardest labors, since it is a law
    set down by yourself that I must earn
    my bread by the sweat of my own brow.
    Give me courage to begin,

patience to go forward,
and ability to finish them.
Cleanse my heart, you who are the Fountain of Purity,
from all falsehood, from all swearing,
from all abuse of your sacred name,
from all foul, loose, and irreverent language.
When I am alone, let my thoughts be of you,
let my mirth in company be to sing psalms,
and let the arguments of my talk
touch only upon the works of your hand.
Take sluggishness from my fingers
and drowsiness from the lids of my eyes;
whether I rise early or lie down late,
let me do it gladly, as if my apprenticeship
were to be consumed in your service.
Thereby, the hourglass of my years shall run out in pleasure,
and in the end I will be made free
in that city of yours, the heavenly Jerusalem;
into whose fellowship, I beseech you,
enfranchise and enroll me; and after
I have faithfully labored six days of my life
here upon earth, may I rest upon the seventh
in your everlasting Sabbath. Amen.

A Prayer for the One Who Buys and Sells

[*Psalm 49:4-7*]

What are all our labors but desperate voyages
    made to purchase wealth? And what are the riches
    of worldly people once they are gotten, but,
    as your prophet sings, "the weaving of a spider's web"?[8]
    The spider makes fine nets to catch flies,
    and the worldly waste their nights
    and wear out their days in tying their consciences
    full of knots to pull up riches.
Since all the travails of our life are like
    buying and selling in a fair,
    which we begin today and end tomorrow—
    so direct my steps, dear Lord, that I may neither
    wander to get goods by unlawful courses,
    nor that I may fall in love with riches,
    however well they be gotten. Let me not
    be one of those buyers and sellers whom your Son Jesus
    thrust out of the Temple, but rather
    one of those merchants who sell all to follow you.
And since to love our neighbor is the fulfilling of the Law,
    give me grace, that I may be counted
    no breaker of that Law, but a keeper of it,
    dealing justly with all people.
And for that purpose, let not my eye look upon false weights,
    nor my hand be held out to take up an uneven balance.
    He loses a piece of his soul—every time—who robs
    the peddler of his measure, and he who gains
    but thirty pence unjustly sells, like Judas,
    even his master, Christ.
As you, O Father of us all, have given me two hands,
    so appoint those servants of my body to execute

none but good and holy offices. Let the one hand
buy honestly and the other sell justly.
Let the left be used to lay up wealth to maintain
my body, and the right to distribute your blessings
to those whose bodies are in misery.
Seal up my lips from lying and forswearing—
the two poisons that overflow every city.
Purge my bosom of corruption,
pull out of my heart the stings of envy,
and let me rejoice to see others prosper
in the world, and not to murmur,
or I myself wither like trees in autumn,
though I lose the golden leaves of wealth
and be left naked with poverty.
Keep the wolf from my door
and the fox out of my bedchamber,
that others may neither lie in wait
to rob me of my goods, nor I sit up late
in the council of the wicked
to deceive others of theirs.
Be at my elbow, O Lord, in all my proceedings,
so I shall fear to do amiss in any.
And so mortify my affections that every day,
casting behind my back the comforts,
the cares, the vanities, the vileness,
the pleasures, and the sorrows of this bewitching world,
that I may continually have this cry aloud in my mouth:
"I desire to be dissolved and to be with you."[9] Amen.

A Prayer for a Chambermaid

[Matthew 25:1–13]

Do not stop up your ears, O Lord, to the requests
    of your poor and humble handmaid,
    in the labors of the body and endeavors of the mind,
    but strengthen me, therefore, O God,
       with your assistance,
    and enlighten my soul with your divine inspiration.
Bestow upon my youth a prosperous flourishing,
    but let it be in goodness. As I grow up in years,
    let me grow up in grace; and write my name,
    O you Eternal Register, in that general pardon
    wherein you forgive the follies of our youth.
Crown me with chaste and religious thoughts,
    and temper my desires so that
    the wanton pleasures of the flesh may not
    drown in me the heavenly treasures of the Spirit.
Take from me, O God, the health of my body
    rather than by the possession of it
    I should grow proud of beauty.
    As long as you account me fair, I care
    not how I appear to the world.
    And though I may be poor, so bless me,
    that I may preserve my character, for
    an honest reputation is an ample dowry to a maiden
Defend me from the poison of evil tongues,
    which are more deadly than the stings of scorpions.
    Defend me from violating those laws
    written down by your own finger.
    Defend me from shame, whose spots
    disfigure the living and disgrace the dead.

Defend me from sin, for the wages
thereof are death and hell.[10]
Make me a faithful steward in ordering
the good of the household I serve, so that
I shall be a more careful disposer of my own.
At my going to rest, take charge of my soul,
for it is your jewel; at my uprising,
guard my body, for your Son has bought it;
so, at the sun's rising, shall I pray to you;
when he is at his height, I will praise you,
and at his going down, I will sing
hymns of thanks to your name—
to which be all honor, for it is due;
all glory, for it is proper;
all fear, reverence, and adoration,
for they are yours alone. Amen.

A Prayer for a Man in Service

[Matthew 25:14-23]

No service, O God, is like that of serving you.
    It is the highway to the highest honor;
    it is a preferment to eternity,
    a promotion beyond that which is bestowed by kings.
    Admit me, therefore, into your household of faith.
    Clothe me in the livery of a true Christian
    so that I shall always wait upon you, O my Lord.
    Lead me away from the company of swearers,
    quarrelers, drunkards, boasters, adulterers,
    and all those who blaspheme you.
Arm me with your grace;
    assist me with your Spirit;
    bless me with your hand;
    fill me with your blessings;
    look down upon my weakness;
    lift me up in strength;
    bear with my frailty;
    suffer not my heart to swell with pride,
    mine eye to burn in lust,
    my tongue to sting with slander,
    my hand to be dipped in blood.
But succor me, O my Maker, and save me—
    oh, save me—now and ever,
    O my Redeemer. So be it. Amen.

A Prayer for a Sailor Going to Sea

[Matthew 8:23-27]

O you, who ride upon the cherubim
 and fly upon the wings of the winds;[11]
 you, at the brightness of whose presence
 the clouds move off, and at whose chiding presence
 hailstones and coals of fire fall upon the world,
 whose arrows are swiftest lightning,
 and whose bow, when it is released,
 shoots forth thunder—be merciful to me, O my God,
 who is about to venture upon the terrors of the deep.
There I will see your wonders, but let me not see your wrath.
 There I will look into hell, but let me not fall
 into the jaws of fear and desperation.
Preserve me, O Lord, in the womb of the ship,
 though the waters climb 'round about its ribs
 to swallow me up, as you did save Jonah
 in the belly of the whale.
 And when, with your servant Peter,
 I cry out to your Son, "Help, Lord,
 or we perish!"[12] let his hand be stretched forth
 to command the waters to be quiet.
Fill our sails with gentle and prosperous winds.
 Let not the sun be covered in storms by day,
 nor the moon and stars conspire with darkness by night,
 to spoil us with shipwreck.
 But set your angel at our helm
 as we hoist sails to go forth,
 and charge that same angel to guide us
 through that wilderness of waters
 till we safely arrive on shore.

Or if, for our sins, it be your pleasure that our bodies
    on this voyage shall perish, yet,
    O our merciful Pilot, save our souls
    from the great Leviathan, whose jaws
    are ever open to devour;
    upon whatever rocks the vessel that bears us
    be split, yet we, most wretched sinners, beg
    at your hands that our heavenly vessels
    may arrive at the everlasting land of promise.
Grant this, O Father. Amen.

A Prayer for Sailors in a Storm at Sea

[Mark 6:47–52]

Save us, oh, save us! Hear the cries of your servants
　　and let them pierce your ear
　　through this battle between the clouds and waters.[13]
　　We perish, O Savior, we perish
　　in this prison of the deep
　　unless by your miraculous power
　　you deliver us from death.
Cast a bridle, therefore,
　　around the stubborn neck of the winds,
　　and beat back this furious army of waters,
　　for they are your slaves. Send us, O Lord,
　　a Moses to conduct us through this Sea of Death.
　　Send but one order
　　in your dreadful and commanding voice,
　　and the tempest will obey you.
You hold the winds in your right hand
　　and the waves in your left;
　　the heavens are your throne
　　and the earth your footstool.[14]
　　All is yours and you are all. To you, therefore,
　　do we fly for succor, because there is no succor
　　except beneath your wings.
The sorrows of death encompass us around;
　　the pains of hell are felt in our bones.
　　Gather, therefore, the seas into a heap,
　　and lay up these storms of wrath
　　in your treasure house of vengeance
　　to confound your professed enemies.

We, simple wretches, call upon your name—oh, hear us!
    We are the work of your own hand—
    oh, deface not your own buildings.
    It was a part of your glory to make us;
    let it be a greater part of your glory to save us,
    now that we are on the point of perishing.
    Save us, oh, save us, for your own sake,
    and we will sing psalms in your praise
    upon the lute and upon an instrument of ten strings.

A Thanksgiving for Sailors' Safe Landing

[Psalm 107:1-6]

Everlasting thanks we pay you—you who are mercy itself,
    for when our feet were stepping into the grave,
    you raised us, like poor Lazarus, from the dead.
Blessed be the God of hosts
    who has redeemed us from danger.
    We were in the lions' den, and yet did he deliver us.
    We were in the furnace, yet not a hair has perished.
    We were at the gates of hell, yet he fetched us back.
    God removed the bitter cup of death from our lips,
    and out of the pit of desperation pulled us up alive.
    He did but say the word,
    and the winds stood still;
    he did but frown,
    and the waters shrunk in their heads;
    he did but beckon,
    and his angel came and brought us comfort.
We will sing, therefore, a song of thanks to our good God.
    We will sound forth his name
    and send abroad the miracle of our deliverance
    to the farthest corners of the earth.
All glory, honor, and praise be yours, O Lord,
    for you are just and without corruption,
    merciful beyond our deserving,
    and mighty above our apprehension.
    All glory, honor, and praise
    be yours, forever and ever. Amen.

A Prayer for a Soldier Going into Battle

[Deuteronomy 20:1]

Arm me, O God of Battles, with courage this day,
 that I may not fall before my enemies.
 The struggle is yours; let the victory be yours.
 Tie to my sinews the strength of David,
 that with a pebble stone I may strike to the earth
 these giants who oppose your truth.
 The weaker the means I use,
 the greater shall be your glory
 if I come from the field crowned with conquest.
 I put no confidence, O Lord, in either
 the strong horse or the iron-headed spear.
 The armor that must defend me is your right arm.
Be my captain, therefore, to conduct me this day;
 let your word be the trumpet to encourage me;
 the banner of the church, the colors that I follow;
 the weapons that I fight with, faith and hope;
 and the cause for which I fight,
 the advancement of true religion.
Keep my hands, O my God, from playing the executioner;
 let pity sit upon my eyelids, even in the heat of battle,
 and let mercy sit on the point of my sword
 when it is most ready to kill.
 Let me fight so that whether I come away
 lame or sound, dead or alive,
 I may live or die your soldier.
Bless me, strengthen me, guide me, guard me,
 save me, O Lord of Hosts. Amen.

A Thanksgiving for a Soldier after Victory

[Psalm 98:1-2]

Vengeance is yours, O Lord, and the fall
   of your enemies is your glory.
   Immortal honor, like the beams of the sun,
   shines around your temples because
   you stood by your poor servant this day.
   You, O Lord, planted a guard of angels around me.
   You circled my brow with the bay tree in sign
   of conquest, and with the palm tree in token of peace.
All that I can give to you for these blessings
   is but the giving of thanks.
   Accept it, O my God, accept this sacrifice of my heart;
   and hold in the reins of my passions so that I be not
   swollen up with arrogance and pride
   about those things that are no work of mine;
   but may I humbly acknowledge you as the author
   of both my own safety and my foe's defeat.
And instruct me in the heavenly discipline
   of other wars I must fight in this world,
   that I may defy Satan and his troops,
   beat down Sin and his damned regiment,
   and triumph over the assaults of the world,
   so that in the end I may march under the banner
   that Christ will spread in heaven. Amen.

A Prayer for a Woman Great with Child

[Psalm 127:3]

Look down from heaven, O Lord, upon me, your handmaid;
 look down from your throne of mercy.
O my God, forget not your servant.
 Forgive me, and so forgive me
 that the child in my body not
 be punished for the mother's offenses.
 Bless this fruit of my womb,
 which you have grafted with your own hand;
 give it growth,
 give it flourishing,
 give it form.
And when the time is come that you will call the child
 out of this close house of flesh,
 where it now inhabits, to dwell
 in the open world, sanctify
 your creature, and on its forehead
 set that sacred seal of baptism,
 that it may be known as a lamb of your own flock.
Grant this, O Redeemer of humankind, at the request
 of your servant and handmaid. Amen.

A Prayer for a Midwife

[Genesis 35:17]

With hands lifted up to heaven,
    knees prostrated on the earth,
    and with a soul humbled at your feet,
    O Lord, I beg you to prosper
    this work I am about to undertake.
    Let me not be fearful in my task,
    fainting in my spirits,
    or too rough in my duty;
    but let me discharge it to your honor
    and to your handmaid's comfort (who is full of pain)
    and to my own credit.
Bless me, O God, with skill, since you
    have placed me as your deputy
    in this great and wonderful business.
    Give your servant an easy and speedy delivery.
    Give me a quick, constant, and gentle hand.
    Give to this unborn creature,
    into whom you have breathed a soul,
    a fair and well-shaped body,
    so that you may have glory by your work;
    and give the mother gladness in beholding
    her infant after all her sorrows.
Grant this, O Father, for your Son's sake,
    Jesus Christ. Amen.

A Thanksgiving after a Woman Delivers Her Child

[Psalm 139:13–16]

Glorified be your name, O God,
 for this mercy extended to your servant.
 It lay in your power to strike death
 into her womb and to heap sorrows upon sorrows,
 but you have given her a double life,
 and you have sweetened her anguishes with gladness.
 Praised be your blessed name;
 praised be your wondrous works.
Continue, O Lord, these your favors to your weak handmaid;
 put strength into her blood,
 blood into her veins,
 and courage into her heart
 so that her lips may render you a thanksgiving.
Look, O God, upon this babe with an eye of love;
 preserve her in health,
 quicken her with your grace,
 and crown her with long life,
 so that she may grow up
 to be a servant in your household.
Untie the strings of this child's utterance when you think it
  proper,
 and give her a tongue that may speak clearly.
 Let all other organs of her body execute their offices
 as you have appointed in your mercy.
Sanctify, O Lord, the breasts
 that must give suck to this babe,
 and, when it pleases you to fill her with understanding,
 feed her soul with the milk of your Word.
Bless us, O Lord, who are here met together
 to behold the glory of your creation

and the wonders of our Creator
in this little infant.
Thanks, honor, and praise be given
to you forever and ever. Amen.

A Prayer for One Who Is Sick

[Matthew 8:7]

Sickness, O Lord, is your herald, I know.
    It is your messenger, and you
        have sent it into my body—welcome
        it is, because it comes from you.
Yet, O my God, if it be your pleasure,
    let your anger cease, and cast
        into the fire that rod which has
        beaten me so long with affliction.
        My soul is brought low, even unto dust.
        Hide not your beams from me, therefore,
        but shed the light of them upon my face,
        that I may lift up my head and be comforted.
You have not yet called me to the bar of death,
    but you have called me to a trial.
        My sins cry out as witnesses against my soul,
        and my soul pleads guilty
        of treason against your majesty.
Restore me, O God, by your pardon,
    under that great seal of your promise,
        to forgive sinners at whatever time
        they heartily pour out their tears of repentance.
Or if it be set down in your book of irrevocable decrees
    that my flesh must with this sickness be turned
        into dust, then strengthen me, O my Redeemer,
        that to the last hour and latest gasp,
        I may hold your name between my lips
        and die with that music as the only sound in my voice.
Grant this request, O Lord, to me your servant;
    that whenever or however the glass
        of my mortality shall run out,

Open the gates of mercy.
Open the doors of your saving health.
Open your arms to receive her in your favor—
or into celestial freedom.
Adopt her as your own.
Adopt her in the blood of your Son, or,
if it is your will, add more days to her life.
Turn, then, speedily her weakness into strength,
and her sickness into health,
so she might confess that you are mighty,
that you are merciful, and that you
alone are the God of salvation.
To you, therefore, who are One in Three,
and Three in One,
and in all things incomprehensible,
be all honor. Amen.

A Prayer for One in Jail

[Psalm 69:33]

My feet, O my Savior, are in the snares of the hunter,
   and like a beast in the wilderness my enemies
   have pursued me. I am now entangled in the chains
   of captivity; yet, O my God, bestow upon me
   the freedom of my soul. Soften the flinty hearts
   of those who have cast me into this house
   of mourning and heaviness; and as you did
   for Daniel in the lions' den, defend and keep
   me from the jaws of misery, which are stretched
   wide open to swallow me up alive.
It is for my sin that I am beset with poverty, shame,
      and dishonor.
   Receive, therefore, these sacrifices of my contrition,
   and do not turn your ear away when my prayers
   are flying toward you. The sighs of the repenting sinner
   are a sweet breath in your nostrils
   and like those tears that washed the feet of Christ.
   Accept, therefore, this offering from the altar
   of a humble, contrite, and wounded heart.
Put into my bosom good and charitable thoughts,
   so that I may pray for those who persecute
   and trouble me, and so that I may undergo
   and pass over all their oppressions
   and bearings of me down, with a settled,
   constant, and suffering spirit.
Let this imprisonment, O Lord, always be to me a book
   in which I may read, first, the knowledge of you,
   which I have previously not studied, and second,
   the knowledge of myself. Let it be a mirror
   in which I may see all the blemishes of my youth—

infuse into me your grace,
teach my tongue to speak of you boldly,
my thoughts to meditate upon you sincerely,
and strengthen my body to maintain your cause
even to the death. Amen.

A Prayer for Those Who Work in Dangerous Places, as Coal Pits, Mines, Etc.

[2 Corinthians 1:8–11]

Out of my bed (the image of my grave)
    you have raised me, O Lord;
    your angels sat upon my eyelids like sentinels
    to guard me while I lay asleep—
    oh, let the same watchmen protect me now I am awake.
Always do I need your help
    (for who can ever be without you?),
    but so near to the house of danger must I dwell this day,
    that on my knees I entreat you to remain
    side by side with me in my goings.
Save my body, O Lord, because, at every turn, Death
    is at my elbow. Whatever happens to my body,
    save my soul, which is the divine part of me,
    so that it may come into your heavenly treasure-house.
Inspire me with that wisdom that descends from above.
    Purify my thoughts and let them, with spotless wings,
    be continually flying around your throne.
Purge my heart, that it may come before you
    like a bridegroom full of chaste love.
    Refine my soul that, like silver
    seven times tried in the fire, it may bear
    the bright figure of salvation
In vain does the builder lay his foundation
    unless your hand is at the setting up.
    Set, therefore, your hand to this work
    of mine, encourage me to undertake it,
    embolden me to go forward,
    and enable me to finish it. Amen.

A Prayer for One Who Is Poor

[*Psalm 10:17–18*]

O King of both heaven and earth, whose blessings
    fall like showers of rain,
    open the rich fountain of your grace
    and let one drop of it relieve me, who is
    the most miserable of your blessed creatures.[19]
You have clothed me in the clothing of baseness, but,
       O Lord,
    furnish my mind with the riches of your mercy.
    I am content, O Father, with this poor estate,
    and I comfort myself with it, knowing
    that your blessed Son had at his birth
    a manger instead of a cradle to lie in and,
    being the Lord of the whole world, not so much
    as a dwelling house of his own to lodge in.
The sparrow does not light upon the ground without your
      providence,
    nor do the lowliest of your children breathe
    without your providing for them.
    Since I came naked into the world,
    this nakedness of mine
    is but the badge of my nativity; bestow, therefore,
    your grace upon me, so that I may not envy
    those who swim in the abundance of wealth.
Feed me, O Lord, with the bread of life,
    so that I may grow strong in health everlasting;
    let me drink of the benefit of my Redeemer's blood.
    Clothe me, O God, with righteousness, and even though
    you have, in your judgment and to express your glory,
    appointed me to be an outcast among the people
    and to be the dust of the world, yet, O Lord,

cast me not out of your presence,
but for your dear Son's sake, whose blood
bought the beggar as well as the prince,
make me a free citizen in the city of heaven. So be it.

PART TWO

The
Eagle

Prayers of Blessing for the Nation

and All Those Entrusted with Authority

To the Reader

Reader, since you have benefited by being a humble suppliant before God when you stood in need of anything necessary to maintain your own life, so you are bound by duty to your Maker, and by the laws of religion and Christianity, to be an earnest suitor to God's Majesty in behalf of others. Since even the most righteous person upon earth still sins seven times a day, and rulers and magistrates, who are set over others, are but human themselves, God has appointed you to make intercession for them, because it is the Lord's custom to lay blessings upon one person through the faithful and zealous prayers of others.

This, briefly, is the task that the King of Heaven and Earth has trusted you with. Read over this book, and it will teach you how to execute this duty and, by discharging it, how to be a true Christian. Do so. You know your reward. Farewell.

A Prayer Offered by the Late Queen Elizabeth

[Psalm 21:7]

O God, all-Maker, Keeper, and Guider,
　　we now engender the boldness to crave,
　　with bowed knees and a heart of humility,
　　your large hand of helping power.
Assist us in our just cause, which is not founded on pride
　　nor begun in malice but is grounded
　　in our just defense from wrongs, from hate,
　　and from the bloody desire of others to conquer us.
Since you have imparted to us the means of preserving
　　all that you have given this nation—
　　by enjoying the people of this country
　　and scorning their bloodshed—
　　we ask for this assurance:
　　Fortify their hearts, dear God,
　　that even their weaknesses may be strengths,
　　that the truest results may spring
　　even from their worst intentions,
　　with the least loss to such a nation of those
　　who sacrifice their lives for our country's good.
May all foreign lands praise and admire
　　the omnipotence of your work—
　　a task that only you can perform.
　　So shall your name be spread abroad
　　for the wonders that you wrought,
　　and so shall the faithful be encouraged
　　to rest in your often unfollowed grace.
And may we, who sought only to do what
　　was right, be chained in your bonds

Crown his middle age with a great number of years,
    as you have crowned his youth
    with the inheritance of many kingdoms.
    Let the dial of his life move slowly on,
    and do not let the last hour of his old age
    strike until those who now stand up
    around him like the tender branches
    of the vine may be seen growing on the banks
    of his kingdom like so many rows of tall cedars.
Let his reign, O Lord, be like the age of Methuselah;
    his knowledge like the wisdom of Solomon,
    and his offspring blessed
    like the seed of Abraham.
    Give him David's soul, but
    do not let him fall into David's sins.
Let him number his people, not to make you angry
    with him but to make him love them.
    Tie, O God, all the strings of their hearts
    to his bosom, like so many lines
    drawn to one center. So shall their safety
    be his fortress, their prosperity
    his riches, and the hours of his pleasure
    the sweetest of their contentment.
Grant these and all other blessings fit
    for such a prince—grant them, O Lord,
    for the benefit of your church,
    for the honor of this kingdom,
    and for the peace of your people. Amen.

A Prayer for the Queen

[Psalm 128:3]

Shed, O Lord, your graces, in showers of abundance,
    upon your royal handmaid, Anne,[2]
    the wife of our sovereign, your servant,
    and the mother to many nations
    besides the glory of her own.
Continue in her that great and excellent work
    that you have begun, though it was
    hidden from our eyes for a number of years.[3]
    That work is, to our kingdom, the best
    and only comfort, which, for the present
    and for the hopes of future ages,
    we do now enjoy—that is, a long, fair,
    and certain line of succession,
    of which we stood doubtful before now,
    though in the secrets of your wisdom
    we were not deprived of it.
As she is now a mother to a heap of scions
    who were born to be kings and queens,
    so, O Lord, make her a grandmother
    to the sons of kings and queens,
    that they may stand around her
    like so many crowned rulers of nations,
    and she in the midst of them,
    as the only tree upon which
    those nations have been grafted.
Let, O God, such an even thread of love
    be spun between her and the king
    that all her thoughts may be confined
    to his bosom and all his desires
    may sleep only upon her pillow,

and that both their hearts may burn
in holy flames of affection toward you.
Sanctify her womb, that it might bring forth
only such fruit as might glorify your name,
shine as sunbeams to comfort this land,
and be as rich jewels in the royal eyes of the parents.
Keep treason, O Lord, from the throne upon which she sits,
and parasites, who are as dangerous as traitors,
from her princely ear when she needs counsel.
Support her by your right hand when she walks forth,
and let your angels go before her at her returning home.
As you have crowned her with happiness
in this world, so when it is your pleasure
for her to take off the robe of mortality,
grant, O Father, that she may be crowned
with stars, and clothed in a robe
of righteousness and of heavenly eternity. Amen.

A Prayer for the Prince of Wales

[Ecclesiastes 10:17]

What are kings, O Lord, unless you
    stand by them as their guard?
    And what are the sons of kings
    unless you vouchsafe to be their Father?
Let the arms of your love, therefore,
    be thrown around that hopeful
    and royal heir to our country,
    Prince Henry.[4] Adopt him
    into your favor. Cover him
    with your wings. Let him be
    to you the apple of your eye.
As yet he is but a green plant.
    Oh, drop the dew of your grace
    upon his head, so that he may flourish
    till the shadow of his branches
    be a comfort to this whole land.
Breathe wisdom into the souls of those
    who are set over him as tutors
    and guardians, that knowledge may,
    as it were, from so many pipes
    be conveyed to his breast,
    and that from there again
    (as from a fountain) it may flow
    clearly and abundantly in all the parts
    of this, your church and kingdom.
Let religion be the column upon which
    he shall always stand, zeal
    the pillow upon which he shall kneel,
    and the defense of the gospel, for which
    he shall go to war. Knit, therefore,

O Lord, strength to his right arm,
and when a good cause calls him into the field,
gird about his loins the sword of victory.
No music, O Lord, is more pleasing to your ear
(as your kingly prophet David sings)
than the unity of brethren.
It is like the precious ointment
that ran down from the head
to the beard, even to the beard
of Aaron, and so to the skirts
of his clothing. Yea, it is like the dew
of Hermon, which fell upon the hill of Zion.
Tune, therefore, O merciful God,
all the heartstrings of this,
our young Prince Henry, and the rest
of that royal blood, his brothers and sisters,
that they may never sound in discord.
Subscribe to these requests of ours, O God,
for your mercy's sake.
Seal them up under the patent
of your promise for your Son's sake,
Jesus Christ, in whose name
whatsoever we ask you have
vowed to grant.
Grant this, give this, O God,
we beseech you.
Amen. Amen.

A Prayer for the Council

[Proverbs 11:14]

Counsel to a kingdom is like the compass
    to a ship under sail; without the one,
    a state is shaken by every tempest,
    and without the other, people run upon
    the rocks of inevitable danger.
Therefore, set your foot, O God,
    among the lords of our council.
    Sit at the table with them,
    and let no decrees pass but those
    in which you have had a hand.
Appoint providence to dwell upon their brows,
    so that they may foresee your enemies and ours.
    Bid watchfulness to sit on their eyelids
    to meet the stroke when it is coming,
    and courage to buckle armor to their breasts,
    so that they may valiantly bear it off
    without shrinking. Let zeal and integrity
    go on either side of them to make them walk upright,
    while concord holds them hand in hand
    to preserve them from factions.
    Give them long life with much honor.
    Heap upon them wisdom with much love.
As they are one body in council, so let all their councils
    be to the safety of one head. Grant this,
    you who weighs all the actions
    of rulers and princes upon earth. Amen.

A Prayer for the Nobility

[Proverbs 25:6–7]

Look down, O Lord, from heaven upon this land
    and upon all those who live here,
    whom we beseech you to bless.
    Pour upon our nobility the riches
    of all your graces. Since every good person,
    O Lord, is noble in your sight,
    so make every person who is noble
    among us also to be good.
Teach them to know that greatness of blood
    is given them so that they should build
    upon it to the greatness of your glory.
    And since they are the fairest streams
    that beautify this kingdom, preserve them,
    O Lord, from the poison of ambition,
    of envy against one another,
    and from dissension.
Stand before the gates of their houses,
    that no foul thoughts or acts may enter
    to stain their families with the spots of treason.
    But be the pillar to uphold them—because
    if you forsake them, the foundation of their houses
    must fall, and their posterity be rooted from the earth.
Guide them, therefore, with your grace,
    arm them with your fear,
    assist them with your love.
    So be it. Amen.

A Prayer for the Church

[*1 Kings 8:13–21*]

The church, O God, is the school where your own laws,
    written in your own hand, are taught.
    It is the temple where you yourself
    utter your divine oracles.
    It is the house where you dwell.
    It is the palace where, with spiritual eyes,
    we behold the brightness of your majesty.
Give it illumination, therefore, by the beams of your glory,
    and since it is your spouse, let her stand
    before you as a virgin, chaste and undefiled.
Drive all foxes and ravening wolves out of this,
    your temple, and allow none but lambs,
    clothed in purity and innocence of life,
    and your chosen flock to feed there.
Let it not be (as it was when your blessed Son
    walked upon the earth) a den of thieves,
    but (as he did, do so also) drive out
    all those who sell your honor
    and the souls of your people.
O Lord, weed this great and universal garden
    of yours of all thorns and briars
    that seek to choke the good seed.
    Plant in it none but seedlings
    of your own nursery, so that you will be sure
    they will bring forth fruit, fair to look at,
    sweet to taste, wholesome for use,
    and such as shall bud out in due season—
    so shall your name be truly honored,
    your praises duly sung, your works,
    with reverence, wondered at, and your wonders

magnified from one end of the world to the other.
Grant that it may be so, for the fullness
    of your Son's merits, and for
    the setting forth of your own mercies. Amen.

A Prayer for the Clergy

[1 Timothy 3:1–16]

Everlasting King of Glory, who sends the ministers
    of your Word as your ambassadors,
      to deal with us about the peace of our souls,
      give them, O Lord, such instructions that
      they may deliver their messages boldly, uprightly,
      and to the good of both your kingdom
      and those to whom they are sent.
They are the heavenly heralds who run
    on errands of our saving health.
    They are angels who go and come
    between you and us. Guide, therefore,
    their feet, that sin may lay
    no stumbling blocks before them
    to make them fall; nor that, forgetting
    the high honor in which you
    have placed them, they be cast down
    for their pride into the pit of darkness.
And since, O God, you have placed them
    on your holy hill, the church, as beacons,
    give them grace, that (like the five wise virgins)
    their lights may never go forth
    without burning brightly to arm your people
    against the invasion of that enemy of humankind,
    the devil and his army, who day and night
    seek to devour them.
Wipe away all mists of errors from their eyes,
    that, seeing you clearly, they may teach
    others how to behold you truly.
They are pastors over your flocks.
    As they have the name of "shepherd,"

so let them have the natures to feed
the sheep committed to their charge,
and not to fleece them.
And as they break for us the Bread of Life
(which you send, employing them
as your stewards, or almoners
of your household), so grant, O Lord,
that we may not allow them to starve
for earthly bread, but that like brothers
we may relieve them, like children
we may reverence them, like lambs of your fold
we may love the shepherds of your fields,
and like sworn soldiers to the cross of Christ,
we may live and die with them
under his glorious banner. Amen.

A Prayer for the Judges of the Land

[Psalm 82:3–5]

Judgment, O Lord, is yours, yet
    to keep us in awe, you have appointed
    judges as your deputies on earth,
    to punish those who go beyond their bounds.
    Give steady hands, therefore, to those
    who hold the sword of justice,
    that they may not strike innocence,
    and that when they need to punish,
    they might imitate you, who smites
    not to kill but to bring about correction.
Let not the left hand of our judges know
    what the right hand does;
    let not the ear near to which the rich man
    stands be opened until the poor man's
    wrongs be both heard and redressed.
O Lord, whip bribery away from their gates
    and partiality out of their private chambers;
    let your laws lie before them when they read
    the statutes of men's making, so that
    in reading what you have written,
    they may not open their lips to pronounce
    false judgment. But sit, O Lord, so close
    to them upon their seats of justice
    that they will recall that they themselves
    must be called one day to judgment,
    so they may do nothing here
    but what, with good conscience,
    they may answer to there. Amen.

A Prayer for the Court

[Proverbs 8:14–16]

O Lord, be a husband to that great household of our king;
    be a father to that family and keep them
    as children both in fear and in love of you.
And because the courts of princes are the very lights
    of kingdoms, pour the oil of your grace
    into this lamp of yours, that it may not
    be darkened but may bring comfort to
    all your people.
Preserve those who live there in brotherly affection
    toward one another and in loyalty
    to him who is their sovereign.
    Banish from there all those vices
    that commonly blemish the beauty
    of kings' palaces; and let your word
    be of such power in this place
    that it may seem to be the temple
    of the everlasting King of Heaven
    rather than the dwelling house
    of a king upon this earth.
Grant this, O Lord, and whatever else
    is requisite for the setting forth
    of your glory, we beseech you,
    in the name of your Son, Jesus Christ.
    Amen.

A Prayer for the City

[Luke 19:41–44]

O Father of mercy, look down upon this city not
    with an eye of justice, for no flesh
    is righteous in your sight, but behold this,
    your sanctuary, as your Son beheld Jerusalem.
Set, O Lord, a host of angels at the gates,
    and let truth spread her banner on the walls.
    Let not the arrow of the invader fall
    upon our houses by day nor the sword
    of the strong man smite us by night.
Give wisdom, O Lord, to the rulers of this city,
    zeal to the preachers, and holiness of life
    to the inhabitants. Let the tree of your gospel,
    which for so many years has flourished here,
    still spread into large branches, and may
    those branches bear an abundance of lively fruit.
Save, O Lord, this temple of yours; bless it, defend it,
    crown it with honors so that it may outshine
    all the cities in the world
    in goodness as it does in greatness. Amen.

A Prayer for the Countryside

[*Matthew 6:28–34*]

You, who are the Creator of all things that are good
    for us, give to our cornfields fatness and increase,
    and to our meadows rain down the waters of plenty.
    Let our land be like that which you said
    should flower with milk and honey,
    for as the heavens are yours, so is the earth yours.
You have also made the north and the south—the winds
    are in your hand. Bridle them, therefore,
    and bind them in the prisons of the earth,
    so that they may not come forth
    to destroy the labors of the plowman,
    nor defeat the husbandman of his hopes.
Raise up faithful and learned and watchful shepherds
    over the poor flock of us, your people, so that
    the blindness of ignorance may not cause our souls
    to wander in the shades of everlasting death.
Guide us, O Lord, neither in the paths of our forefathers
    (if they went astray) nor in the common steps
    of the present time, unless it be according
    to those ways that were trod out before us
    by your Son Jesus Christ.
Teach us to love you, to know you, to live after your laws,
    and to die after your commandments;
    so we shall be sure to exchange this country of frailty,
    of sin and misery, for the land of promise
    and the kingdom of all fullness and felicity.
Grant this, O Father of us all, grant this,
    O Redeemer of us all. Amen.

A Prayer for a Magistrate

[Romans 13:1–3]

O Lord, you have called me (of the earth
    and raised to riches, even out of the dust)
    to be a ruler over others.
    Bestow on me, therefore, the spirit of wisdom,
    that I may first learn how to govern myself,
    for the perfect knowledge of ourselves
    brings us, O God, to the true knowledge of you.
O my Maker, in this summit of my height, with my head
    being lifted up to honor, humble me so that
    my heart may not swell up with pride.
    Give me a mind to execute not my own will
    but yours. Give me an eye that may not lust
    after my own profit but seek the advancement
    of your glory and the good of the commonwealth.
As you have placed me to be a pillar to uphold others,
    grant that I may not prove a weak pillar,
    to throw myself down and, with my fall,
    bruise others that stand under me.
In all my ways, O Lord, go before me as a lantern
    to my feet. In all my actions, stand by me
    as my schoolmaster to direct me.
    In all my prosperity, let me look only upon you.
    In all my troubles of body or mind,
    turn not your eyes from me.
O Savior, let me not forget you in the abundance of wealth,
    nor fall into despair and forsake you in poverty.
Grant this and whatever else, O Lord, I stand in need of
    in order to guide me in this dangerous sea,
    where you have appointed me to sail.
    Grant it, O God, for your Son's sake,
    in whose name I beg your mercies. Amen.

A Prayer for a Lawyer

[Micah 6:8]

O you, who are the truest Lawgiver, instruct me
    in the holy decrees of your Word
    so that I may practice nothing
    but the fulfilling of your ordinances.
    Let not my tongue plead and be employed
    with purchasing earthly goods for others
    and be forgetful of how to provide
    for the salvation of my own soul.
As my profession is the law, so let my profession
    be to do right for all people, for equity
    is the ground upon which law is built.
Take from my bosom, O Lord, all immoderate
    and unmeasurable desires of heaping up
    the riches of this world together
    by unlawful means. Let me not,
    by oppression, join house to house,
    land to land, and lordship to lordship,
    but may I ever remember that I am but
    as a pilgrim upon earth, and that
    at my departure from here I must go
    either to eternal glory
    or to endure torment without end.
Grant, therefore, O my God, that I may deliver
    to all people their true Ephah and their true Hin,[5]
    that is to say, their just measure of that
    which, of right, belongs to them.
O Lord, give me (as your kingly prophet begged
    from your hand) neither poverty nor abundance
    of wealth; only grant me so much

as may maintain my life. For your Son's sake,
my Redeemer, hearken, O Lord,
to these requests of your servant. Amen.

A Prayer for the Universities

[*Proverbs 2:1-5*]

O you, who are the unsearchable depth of all wisdom,
   open the fountain of knowledge,
   and let the streams of it run
   to the nurseries of learning,
   that from the breasts of those
   (as it were, from the tender nipples
   of mothers) the youth and gentry of this land
   may suck the milk of both divine and human science.[6]
Graft, O Lord, onto those great trees infinite numbers
   of plants, that in good time they may yield much fruit
   to profit your church and the public welfare.
And seeing that these stars of learning are meant
   to give comfort, or to fill the darkness in this,
   our whole kingdom, bestow upon them, O Lord,
   such beams of heavenly light that even foreign countries,
   as well as our own, may be glorified in their splendor.
Direct all the studies of those who live upon the food
   of the soul there (which is wisdom) to a holy end.
   Make them to love each other as brothers
   and to live as Christians; let not vainglory
   engender pride among them, nor fancifulness
   of wit drown them in ridiculous and apish folly.
But so mold both their minds and bodies that they may enter
   into those sanctified temples as children and go
   from there as servants of your ministry. Amen.

A Prayer for the Confusion of Those Who Would Harm Our Nation by Violence

[Psalm 3:7]

O Father of Nations, O King of Kings and Lord of Lords,
    send from your throne a host of angels to guard
    our prince, his realm, and his people
    from the devouring jaws of the violent,
    which are stretched wide open to swallow up
    this land where your gospel is taught and practiced.
Arm us with safety and with boldness, that we,
    without fear of peril, may walk upon the lion
    and the adder that lies in its den, waiting to suck
    our blood. Yea, cover us, O God, with your wings,
    that we may tread upon the young lion and the dragon
    that spits fire to destroy this noble kingdom
    and to drink the blood of your anointed.
May the death of Saul fall upon those who persecute
    your servant David; let David, O Lord, escape,
    but let these Sauls perish by the sword.
    May the misery that struck the house of Jeroboam,
    because he caused Israel to sin, be girded around
    these enemies of your church and our country.
O God, in your just wrath, smite the rocks
    and send the whirlwinds forth to blow the dust
    of their wicked counsels into their own eyes.
    Give to these Ahithophels the shame and confusion
    that Ahithophel met with in his cursed treasons
    with Absalom against his father, David;
    yea, O Lord, let the proudest of the faction
    die upon a tree as proud Absalom did.
Rise up, Lord, and with the breath of your nostrils
    disperse into air all these conspiracies;

scatter the violent as chaff
tossed before the wind. Bring to light
whatever they plot in darkness, and let
their own counsels be their own confusion. Amen.[7]

A Prayer in Time of Civil War

[Psalm 85:4–6]

Heavy are our sins and many in number, and never
    do we run out in tallying them, not thinking
    upon the last dear and most dreadful account
    to which one day we must be called.
Our sins are great in quantity, yet they have a quick pace
    and are ever at our heels, no matter how fast
    we fly from them, so that if your justice, O God,
    pursues us, we are but like sheep running
    to slaughter or as soldiers felled to the earth
    in the day of battle. Have mercy, therefore,
    O God of all mercy; pull in the rod of your anger,
    and take pity on us, your children.
    Smite us not in your rage, for then we perish,
    but chasten us in your love, and then we shall amend.
But above all the punishments that you have laid up
    in store for us, and that we all deserve, defer,
    O God, defer, yes—swear you will not hew down
    this land (as the harvester's sickle mows
    the corn) with the iron rod of civil war.
Beat back the waves that would drown their own shores
    to whom they owe obedience, and let them
    serve to quench any fires that by rebellious hands
    shall be kindled to burn in the bosom of our kingdom.
For a long time, O Lord, we have been onlookers of
    our neighbor countries and have seen
    their cities turned to cinders, and yet we
    have not been scorched with the flames.
Oh, send not your angel with a fiery sword from them
    to us, to make them spectators of our misery,
    nor to shake it over our cities, as you did when you

threatened destruction to your own city, Jerusalem.
Spare us, O Lord, and look not upon us in the day
of indignation. Save us from the arrows
of other nations, and let not the hands
of our own people be our own murderers.
For the sake of your Son, Jesus Christ, who lost
his blood that we might not be cast away,
do we beg this. Grant this, O Lord.
Amen, now and forever, amen.

A Prayer to Withhold the Pestilence

[Psalm 91:1-3]

O Lord, withhold the invader's arm, who shoots darts
    of pestilence so thickly among us that we
    descend into the merciless grave in heaps.
Death is but your servant and can execute none
    but those whom you condemn, yet he has played
    (and still does play) the cruel tyrant;
    for the living whom he spares are not able
    to bury the carcasses as fast as he destroys them.
Check him, therefore, O God, and charge him no more
    to spoil these temples made by your own hands.
    O God of heaven, we have broken your laws—
    we confess as much. We repent that we
    have angered so good and gracious a Father.
O Son of God, we have crucified you again and again
    with our sins, we confess. We repent that we
    have abused so excellent an author
    of our redemption; yet have mercy upon us.
O Father, speak in our behalf. O blessed Son, plead
    for our pardon. Be our mediator, reconcile us
    to the King of heaven and earth,
    against whom we have committed treason.
And whatever becomes of our bodies, no matter
    how soon they must turn into earth, yet
    have mercy on our souls, save them,
    O Savior, challenge them to be your own,
    and lay them up in the treasure-house of heaven
    because they are the jewels bought
    with the price of your precious blood. Amen.

A Prayer in Time of Famine

[Ezekiel 36:26–30]

Three whips, O Lord,
    destroy the mightiest nation—
    war, pestilence, and famine.
    The last of them is the worst,
    the sharpest, and the most terrible.
O merciful God, wind up the cords of this,
    the most dreadful executioner;
    bind up the jaws of this insatiable vulture,
    that she may not breathe upon the people;
    but open the entrails of the earth,
    that she may give to humans and beasts
    their wanted sustenance.
As you have made mouths, so make meat
    to fill those mouths; otherwise, Christians
    will feed upon the blood of Christians,
    as has been done before in other kingdoms
    that have fallen from your obedience.
Avert, O Lord, this consuming plague from the gates
    of our cities, and instead of penury,
    send plenty to relieve us.
    Make us thankful for your blessings,
    and let us not repine at your punishments,
    but with patience bear willingly
    whatever you lay upon us—and yet,
    O Father, lay no more than flesh and blood
    may suffer, and let all that you do
    be only for our trial and amendment. Amen.

A Prayer in Time of Persecution

[2 Timothy 3:10–12]

O Lord, from the beginning,
    wolves and ravenous beasts
    have broken into your pastures
    and sucked the blood of your sheep;
    now, even now, the traps are set.
Arise, therefore, from your throne and set
    your foot on the proud, stiff necks
    of these persecutors of your gospel
    and scoffers of your glory.
Strike them, O Lord of Hosts, with your right arm,
    and make them blind in their own works;
    and as you did at the building of Babel,
    confound the pride of your enemies
    by altering their languages; O God,
    cast down this Babel of idolatry.
Be our God and save your people whom
    your Son has redeemed.
    Be our captain and fight for your church,
    which your Son has called his spouse.
So shall we, your people, worship you freely;
    so shall we triumph to see
    your honor advanced;
    so shall we ever praise you;
    so shall the nations glorify your name. Amen.

A Prayer for the Head of a Family

[*Proverbs 23:22–25*]

O Lord, since you have made me a steward
    over a family, direct me
    by your own laws, so that I
    may never step beyond the limits
    of my duty, with the intention
    that when I am called to account
    on that great audit day, according
    to how I behaved myself in that office,
    I may receive from you, O Lord,
    the wages of a faithful servant.
O Father of heaven and earth,
    bless the labors of my own hand
    and of those who are committed
    to my charge. Let me not descend
    into base and indirect ways
    to purchase riches, but, according
    to your own statute, with the sweat
    of my brow, let me eat my bread.
Inspire me with knowledge of your holy Word,
    so that I may learn how to live well,
    and I may instruct those
    around me to do likewise.
Temper, O Lord, my mind and affections,
    that no household squabbles
    may be kindled under my roof;
    or, if they catch fire, give me patience
    to endure them and wisdom
    to know how to quench them.
Preserve my name, O my God,
    that I never enter into any action

that might dishonor you or bring
   my own life into infamy.
At my uprising, bless me.
   At my down-lying, lay your hand over me.
   In my walks, be my guide.
   In my meditations, be my tutor.
Let your Book be my study, and let all
   my study be to find advancement
   among those who are chosen
   for everlasting life, to which, O Lord,
   bring me, I most humbly beseech you,
   for your own glory's sake and for
   your Son's sake, Jesus Christ. Amen.

PART THREE

The
PELiCAN

Prayers of Supplication to Christ to Help Us

Overcome the Seven Deadly Sins

To the Reader

The third bird that I call out of Noah's ark is the Pelican. The nature of the Pelican is to peck her own bosom and with the drops of her blood to feed her young ones. Christ, the Son of God, is the Pelican whose blood was shed to feed us. The physician made a medicine of his own body to cure us. Look upon him well, and behold his wounds bleeding, his head bowed down (as if to kiss us), his very sides opened (as if to show how his heart loved us), his arms stretched out to their length (as if to embrace us). And judge by all these if Christ be not our truest Pelican.

He who was King of Heaven and Earth suffered his brow to wear a crown of thorns. He received wounds that are our health. He tasted the bitterness of death that is our only salvation—what Pelican can do more for her young ones?

Our souls were spotted: Sin had pawned them, sin had lost them, sin had made them foul. All the medicine in the world could not purge our corruption, all the fountains in the world could not wash our spots, all the gold and silver on earth could not redeem our forfeitures, all the kings under heaven could not pay our ransoms. Nothing could free us from captivity but to make Christ a prisoner. Nothing could give us life but the heavenly Pelican's death. Our evil actions were the judges that should have called us to the bench. Conscience was the evidence that should have cast us away; and sins were the executioners who were to be our tormentors.

But note the mercy of our Maker, note the courage of our Redeemer. Against seven deadly and detestable sins—which came into the field (to set upon all the children of Adam) in that great battle and work of our salvation—came Christ, armed with seven lively virtues. Thus was his combat, and thus was his victory.

He suffered himself to be betrayed by a Judas; there fought his humility and overcame pride.

He left not our safety till he had lost his own life; there fought his love and overcame envy.

He took buffets on the face, scourges on the back, pricking briars on the forehead; there fought his patience and triumphed over wrath.

He was ready in all tempests to throw himself overboard to save us from shipwreck; there fought his watchfulness and slayed the sin of sloth.

He gave away himself and the world, so that the world to come might by his Father be given to us; there fought his liberality and overcame covetousness.

He drank of the sourest and bitterest grape so that we might taste of the sweetest; there fought his temperance and over gluttony got the conquest.

He could not be tempted with all the kingdoms upon earth nor all the pleasures in those kingdoms; there fought his continence and overcame lust.

Thus with the seven blows did he strike off the heads of seven dragons that stood gaping to devour us. We are still in danger of them; let us therefore arm ourselves with those weapons that Christ has taught us to handle in our own defense, and those are these that follow.

A Prayer for the Morning

[Psalm 5:1-3]

When I rise from my bed, O my Redeemer,
    it puts me in mind of my rising from the grave,
    when the last trumpet shall sound and summon us
    to the general resurrection. Then I hope
    to behold you coming in the fullness of your glory,
    and your Father sitting in the brightness of his majesty,
    and that I shall have a place among those
    who are written in your Book of Life.
So, O my Mediator, make intercession for me,
    so that all the sins of my former days
    and nights being freely pardoned, I may
    this day be welcomed into your service.
Receive, therefore, O Lord, this early sacrifice
    both of my soul and my body.
    I offer them up into your hands
    to be disposed of at your pleasure,
    and with them, I offer unfeigned sighs
    for having offended you, and with those sighs
    my zealous prayers for your pardon,
    and with those prayers an assured hope,
    that in your mercy and in the blood
    of that loving Pelican, Christ Jesus,
    who died for me, I shall be forgiven.
    Blessed be your name for blessing
    me this night from danger.
I read in the Book (written by your own finger)
    that you cast Adam into sleep
    when you made a woman from his rib;[1]
    by this I note that man of himself
    has no power to bind slumber

to his temples unless you give it to him.
All thanks, therefore, be yours, that this night
　　has covered me with the soft wings
　　of quietness and so, graciously, does now
　　allow me to behold the light of the day.
Go on, O God, with your favors toward me,
　　your humble servant; go along beside me
　　and with me all this day, and all the days
　　of my life; that I may not step into the path of sin.
Grant this, I beseech you, give me your grace
　　and forgive me my debts, which I owe
　　to sin and death. So be it. Amen.

A Prayer against Pride

[Proverbs 11:2]

O Son of the everlasting God, who even at your birth
    called Joseph your father, and in your cradle,
    which was but a poor manger, and who in the height
    of all your passions and sorrows upon the cross
    was the true pattern of true humility—teach me, O Lord,
    to tread that path in all my tribulations.
    Make me your student, and leave me not
    until I have that lesson perfectly by heart.
While God, your Father, is, over all the world, the highest,
    it is to express divine majesty. You (who are God's Son),
    of all those who are in your fold, are the lowliest minded;
    but that is to instruct us, your children, in obedience.
For, alas, what reason have I to be proud?
    Am I not dust and ashes?
    Am I not made of the clay of the earth?
    And must I not, in the end, like a potter's
    earthen vessel, be broken all into pieces?
Your prophet Amos told the people that you hated even
    the pride of Jacob, and abhorred his palaces.[2]
    And can I have any hope (not being as dear
    to you as Jacob) that you can love
    to behold that serpent of pride
    with seven heads sleeping in my bosom?
    Now your hand is armed against the hand of
    the proud, who cannot escape confusion.
Pride was the first sin that crept into the world;
    but so ugly a sin it was that it could not be allowed
    to stay in heaven, for Lucifer, the father of sin,
    from the glory of an angel was thrown headlong
    (for his insolence) into the pit of hell.

Pharaoh was proud, but Pharaoh
    and his host fell in their pride.
    Sennacherib was proud, but Sennacherib
    was trod upon by the feet of his own children.
    Haman was proud, but his end was
    the gallows tree, which he set up for another.
Yea, so odious a monster in your eye, O God,
    is a proud man that proud Nebuchadnezzar,
    being a king, was by you turned into a beast
    and ate grass till he confessed himself
    to be but a man, and that you only, O God,
    were the God of heaven and earth.
And on the contrary side, so precious a jewel
    is humility in your sight that none
    could be Christ's disciples but such
    as wore the garments of lowliness.
Pull down, therefore, O Lord—nay, pull up
    by the very root this tree of pride
    if you perceive it growing within me.
    Let none of the branches of this sin,
    O God, spread in the world, but lop
    them off even in their budding forth.
    And for that purpose let not vainglory
    (one of the pages of pride) follow learning.
    Let not disdain sit in the eye of greatness
    to cast terrifying looks upon the distressed.
    Let not presumption of your mercies
    make us tempt you to destroy us
    in our security; nor let your long-suffering
    and winking at our sins stir up our souls
    to disobedience and rebellion.
But turn all our affections in such concord
    that we may count our glories but shadows,
    our strength but weakness,

our riches but temptations and snares
to catch up our souls,
our wisdom but folly,
our life but a bubble in water,
and our death but our everlasting journey
to that land of sorrow—unless,
at our setting forth, you undertake
to be the pilot. Be that pilot, therefore,
our merciful God, and despite all the rocks
that sin and her dreadful sea monsters
set in the way for our destruction,
safely set us, we beseech you,
upon the shore of eternal felicity.
Amen, O Lord, amen. So be it
now and forever. Amen.

A Prayer against Envy

[Proverbs 14:30]

O King of Heaven, it is a branch in your heavenly statute
    that we should love our enemies
    and bless those who curse us
    and do good to them who hate us
    and pray for those who lay plots for our lives.
    These are the strings, O God, whose music
    is pleasing to your ear; these are the stairs
    by which we climb up to charity,
    and, holding her by the hand,
    we are led up into heaven.
Purge, therefore, O Lord, our veins
    and let not the stinking poison of envy
    infect our blood, but following in
    the steps of Samuel, let us pray
    for King Saul, even though he
    is an enemy to your servants;
    and like Moses, let us not repine
    at the stubborn Hebrew children, even though
    they rebel and threaten us with death.
Envy, O God, is the destroyer of those
    who nourish it in their bosoms.
    It is the tormentor of one's own self.
You have commanded us to love our neighbors as ourselves;
    but how can we show love to them when,
    while envy is sucking our own blood,
    we suck even the ruin of our own bodies?
    As rust eats the iron, so does this vulture gnaw the soul.
Envy turns us into devils; yea, into worse than devils
    does it turn us. The Pharisees perished
    because they chose to envy Christ and his miracles

rather than to believe him.

Other sins have their limits, but the stream of envy
keeps within no bounds. If pride were barren,
envy would never have been born, but that sin
is the mother of this one, and this sin
is the fountain of ten thousand more.

By means of this sin, the world was drowned,
and by means of this sin was your Son betrayed to death.
Cut it off, therefore, O Lord,
and let not its seed grow in our hearts.
How dare we, O God, ask forgiveness
at your hands when we are out of charity
and wish the downfall of our neighbor?

Therefore, pour your divine grace into our souls
so that we may strive to be like you,
that is, to be all love and all mercy.
So shall we live with you forever.
So shall we die your servants,
and being raised up again,
we shall be your children. Amen.

A Prayer against Wrath

[Ephesians 4:26–32]

Wrath is a short madness;
    madness is the murderer of reason,
    so that anger transforms us into brute beasts.
    Give us courage, therefore, O Lord, to fight against
    this strong enemy, and not only to fight,
    but to overcome him—for it is harder to triumph
    over our raging affections than to subdue a city.
All vengeance is yours, O God, and if we offer
    to take it out of your hand, it is high treason;
    for we do as much as if we set about to pull
    you from your throne. Inspire us, therefore,
    with patience, so that we may bear injuries
    as your Son did upon earth, and may endure
    afflictions (as your servant Job did)
    when it shall please you to send them
    as your messengers, and that we may not
    at any time either murmur against your providence
    or be angry with you for whatever you send,
    be it health or sickness, life or death;
    nor, in the bitterness of our souls, pour down
    curses (which are some of the drops of wrath)
    upon whatever rulers or teachers you set
    over us; lest your heavenly vengeance smite us
    (with Miriam, who murmured against Moses).
But cast, O Lord, such a bridle upon our stiff-necked
        affections
    that all contention, quarrels, bloodshed, war, and murder
    (who are the sons of wrath) may be curbed
    and not allowed to do violence to your church,
    to offer dishonor to your saints,

or disturbance to the commonwealth.
Sign, O Lord, the humble petition of your servants,
    that we may live here like doves
    one to another, without gall;
    and at our departure from here,
    we may mutually embrace
    and hold hands together to meet you in glory.

A Prayer against Sloth

[Ecclesiastes 10:18]

How hateful the sin of sloth is in your eyes, O Lord.
    May we learn from the life of our first father, Adam,
    who, although he had a whole world to himself
    and all things made ready to his hand, yet,
    to teach us that he was not born to live idly,
    you placed him in the garden of Eden,
    and there appointed him to labor.
And even from the beginning have you enacted
    that we should live by the sweat of our brow,
    that we should earn our bread before we taste his bread,
    and that we who would not work should not eat—
    for as a bird is created to fly in the air,
    as fish are to swim in the waters,
    so are we made to take pains upon earth.
What were the sins of Sodom but pride,
    fullness of meat, wealth, and idleness?
    Keep these sins, therefore, O Lord,
    from the gates of our cities lest
    they bring upon us the same confusion.
Have we not examples
    (even of those who were tender to your love)
    that we should not nourish this disease in our blood,
    but that we should spend our lives
    as the clouds execute their offices to be always in
        motion?
Were not Abraham, Lot, Isaac, and Jacob plowmen
        and shepherds?
    Did not your servant Moses keep the sheep of Jethro,
    his father-in-law, the priest of Midian?
    Was not David, before he was anointed king,

a shepherd also? Yea, did not your own Son
take pains continually while he lived among the people?
Were not his apostles fishermen, and did not Luke
(your blessed evangelist
and one of your Son's chroniclers)
practice medicine and painting?[3]
In these men, O Lord, and in their lives
you have set down rules for us to follow.
Put, therefore, strength into our arms,
that we may endure labor.
Kindle our minds with courage
and livelihoods, that in winter we may not
be loath to take hold of the plow
for fear of the cold, lest when summer
comes we fall into beggary.
And above all things, so encourage us with your grace,
and so quicken our understandings with your spirit,
that we may not be dulled and so neglect
the knowledge of your laws,
nor by laziness be besotted with ignorance
and so lose the remembrance of our duties.
O Lord, let not this unprofitable weed of sloth
grow up among the ministers of your Word.
Let no standing waters be in your church,
but give swiftness to them, that they may all
be running streams—so shall your pastures
be watered and bring forth increase;
so shall your flocks be well tended,
when the shepherds be watchful;
so shall we all set our hands to the raising up
of your heavenly tabernacle;
and so, in the end, shall we be lifted up
to sit with you and your Son in heaven. Amen.

A Prayer against Covetousness

[Luke 12:15–21]

O Father of heaven and giver of all blessings,
    open your hand, but only open it
    so that the pouring down of your benefits
    may not make us swell into a desire
    to hoard up more than is fit for us to receive.
The love of worldly honors only makes us
    love the world and forget you.
    The love of gold and silver makes us
    forsake heaven and lose you.
    O let not, therefore, the gripping talons
    of covetousness seize upon our souls.
It is a golden devil that tempts us to hell.
    It is a mermaid whose songs are sweet but full of sorcery.
    It is a sin that turns courtiers into beggars,
    and yet makes them wear monopolies on their backs,
    when the commonwealth shivers through the cold.
    It is a sin that sells your church (by simony)
    and sends souls away at an easy rate.
    It is a sin that blinds the eye of justice.
    It is a bell whose sound so deafens the voice of the poor
    that wrongs against them cannot be heard.
Drive, therefore, this plague out of our land, O Lord,
    and make us covetous of nothing but of your glory
    and of the riches of your gospel;
    let us be covetous of doing well to one another,
    so shall we be sure to stand in favor with you.
A covetous person is like hell, ever devouring, never satisfied,
    an insatiable drunkard of gold.
    Quench, O Lord, this thirst of money in us;
    keep our hands clean from touching riches unlawfully,

lest like Jezebel we commit murder
and shed Naboth's blood, to wring from him his
    vineyard;
or with Achan be stoned to death
for taking goods that are forbidden to us.
Grant these blessings, O Father Almighty, and with them,
    give us grace to be content with such estate,
    however lowly, as you shall lay upon us;
    let the wealth we desire be your kingdom,
    and the gold we thirst after be our salvation. Amen.

A Prayer against Gluttony

[Proverbs 23:20–21]

How many woes, O Lord,
    are thundered out by your prophets
    against this bestial and devouring sin of gluttony?
    "Where is woe?" cries out that proclaimer of all wisdom,
    King Solomon. "Where is wailing? Where is strife?
    Where are snares laid? Where are wounds taken?
    Where are bloody eyes?
    Nowhere but where the drunkard fills up on wine
    and the epicure feeds on his variety of dishes."
Preserve us, O God, from falling into this bottomless gulf.
    You have given all creatures to us to serve our uses,
    but let us not turn to our destruction
    that which was ordained for our comfort.
This sin of intemperance was the sin of our first parents;
    it was a sin of sweetness, but it was sourly
    and severely punished. The eating of an apple
    lost them their Paradise
    and brought your heavy curse upon us.
Strengthen, therefore, our hearts, O God,
    with your grace, not with the fullness of meats.
    Give us the waters of life to taste
    and not strong wines to overcome us—
    since drunkards shall not inherit the kingdom of heaven.
And lastly, set always before our eyes the pictures
    of the rich glutton and of poor Lazarus;
    the one feasted deliciously every day
    and drank of the purest grape,
    but afterward he lay howling in hell
    and could not get a drop of cold water
    to quench his burning thirst.

The other fed upon crumbs, and he
was carried into Abraham's bosom.
To that place, O Lord, send us, and grant
that we may sit at that table of your saints,
where neither hunger not thirst shall afflict,
but where all fullness is found, all gladness,
all riches, all rest, all happiness. Amen.

A Prayer against Lust

[1 John 2:16–17]

My body, O Lord, is a temple consecrated to you.
    Keep it, then, I beseech you, clean and free
    from the pollution of sin; and among all
    who lay siege to destroy it, defend it
    from unbridled flames of lust.
Close up my lips, O God, from speaking unchaste language;
    sanctify my thoughts so that no wanton desires
    may burn in my bosom. Be present in all my actions
    so that no temptations of the flesh
    may lead my soul into wickedness.
The sin of lust, O Lord, is a covetous sin,
    not content with the spoiling of one body
    but working the everlasting perdition of two at once.
    It is a sin so foul that by a specific law
    you have forbidden it in your tablets;
    yea, and you have vowed that the offender
    shall go down to hell, while he
    who flees from it shall be saved.
Place modesty, therefore, in my eye,
    that lascivious glances may not there
    have entrance; let me with Joseph
    rather suffer imprisonment than to make
    anyone a slave to intemperate lust.
It is written upon those records of yours, which cannot lie,
    that so hateful to you, O God, was David's
    adultery with the wife of Uriah
    that even though he was your chosen servant,
    he could not escape your punishment.
Forgive, therefore, the follies of my youth,
    and let my body hereafter be a vessel

of purity, so that at the last day,
when all creatures must stand before you,
I may appear in whiteness and receive that crown
of glory prepared for the blessed. Amen.

A Prayer against the Temptations of the Devil

[1 Corinthians 10:13]

Our life, O Lord, which passes through so dangerous
    a wilderness, cannot choose but meet with many sins.
    Every sin is a temptation. To overcome every temptation
    is a glorious victory, and the reward of that victory
    is an everlasting crown of stars,
    for there can be no conquest without a combat;
    and there can be no combat without an enemy
    to engage with; and no enemy is more ready
    to set upon us, and more subtle in his fight,
    nor more cruel when he subdues,
    than that arch-traitor to your kingdom
    and old enemy to humankind, the Devil.
Give him, therefore, O Lord, no power over me, or,
    if it be your pleasure that I must enter into combat
        with him,
    let my trials be like those of Job,
    to exercise my faith and not to confound my soul;
    to which battle when I must be summoned,
    stand, O my Savior, in my sight to inspire
    me with courage, and plant a guard of angels
    on either side of me to take my part if I shrink;
    that in the end I may be led away in triumph.
Break, O my God, all the snares that daily and hourly
    this crafty hunter pitches to entrap me,
    in the lustiness of my health and youth.
    But above all, let me not fall into those
    that he spreads at the hour of my death
    to catch my soul at her departure.
O Lord, drive away despair, that it may not enter
    at that time, nor at any other, into my bosom;

neither let me be afraid that I knock
at the gates of mercy too late
or distrust your grace, because
so many thousands of sins do muster
themselves before me; but comfort me
with the sweet medicine of your promises,
and with the examples of your holiest servants,
who all sinned grievously, yet you
did seal them with a pardon.
In my meditations stand, O Lord, at my elbow—
that my soul may not wander and be lost.
Defend me from the arrow of death eternal.
Save me from the jaws of the Red Dragon.
Keep me from entering into the gates of hell. Amen.

A Prayer for the Evening

[Psalm 42:8]

Thus, O God, am I nearer to old age
    than I was in the morning,
    but, I fear, not nearer to goodness.
    For he who strives to do best comes short of his duty.
    The night now steals upon me like a thief.
    Oh, defend me from the horrors of it.
When I am to lie down in my bed, let me imagine
    I am to lie in my winding sheet,
    and let me not close my eyes until
    my soul and I have reckoned and made even
    for all the offenses that not only this day,
    but all the former minutes of my life,
    I have committed against your Divine Majesty.
Pardon them, O Lord; forgive me my sins,
    which are more infinite than the stars
    and more heavy than if mountains
    were to lie upon my bosom;
    but your mercy and the merits
    of my Redeemer do I trust in.
    In his name do I sue for pardon.
O Lord, let no unclean thoughts this night
    pollute my body and soul,
    but keep my cogitations chaste,
    and let my dreams be like those
    of innocents and sucking babes.
Grant, O Lord, that the sun may not go down
      upon my wrath.
    But if anyone this day has done me wrong,
    that I may freely and heartily forgive them,
    just as I desire to be forgiven by your hands.

Whether I sleep or wake, give your angels charge over me,
that at whatever hour you call me, I may,
like a faithful soldier, be found ready to encounter Death
and to follow the Lamb wherever he goes. Amen.

PART FOUR

The PhoEnix

Prayers of Thanksgiving for the Benefits We Receive

in the Death and Resurrection of Christ

To the Reader

You have by these three former birds of Noah's ark received three blessings. The Dove ministered comfort to your afflicted mind in a number of those storms of tribulation that fall upon people in this life. The Eagle armed your soul with courage and taught it to soar high with the wings of prayer till they beat at the very gates of heaven and from there received mercy. The Pelican has played the true physician, and, where you are full and foul with diseases bred by sin, it taught the way to cure you and to attain the health of salvation. The fourth bird is now flying out toward you; spread, therefore, your arms wide open to welcome it, and this Phoenix will carry you up and on to a second life that shall be ever, everlasting.

Among all birds, the Phoenix lives the longest—so must our prayers fly up in bright flames all the days of our lives. We must be petitioners even to the last hour and last minute of our breath. The Phoenix has the most beautiful feathers in the world, and prayers are the most beautiful wings by which we may mount into heaven. There is but one Phoenix upon earth, and it has but one tune in which God delights, and that is the prayer of a sinner.

When the Phoenix knows she must die, she builds a nest of all the sweetest spices, and there, looking steadfastly at the sun, she beats her wings in its hottest beams and between them kindles a fire among those sweet spices and so burns herself to death. So, when we desire to die to the vanities of the world, we must build up a nest and fill it with faithful sighs, groans, tears, fasting and prayer, sackcloth and ashes—all of which are sweet spices in the nostrils of the Lord—and then, fixing our eyes upon the cross where the glorious Son of God paid the ransom of our sins, we must not cease till, with the wings of faith and repentance, we have kindled his mercy and in that sweet flame have all our fleshly corruptions consumed and purified. Out of those dead ashes of the Phoenix does a new Phoenix rise. And even so, out of the ashes of that one repentance shall we be regenerate and born anew.

Out of the purest flames of love, Christ kindled a fire that drank up the wrath of his Father, a fire in which all people should have been drowned for their sins, and in that fire did he die to redeem us who were lost. Yet he did not leave it there. To have died for us would have been worth nothing if he hadn't also, like a true Phoenix, been raised up again. As a grain of wheat is cast into the earth and there first rots and then comes to life again and after yields itself in a tenfold measure, so was our Savior cast into his sepulcher, where his dead body lay for a time and then came to life again and then was raised up. And in that rising did he multiply those benefits that before he sowed among us, when he was torn in pieces and scattered on the cross.

When he died, he died alone, but when he did rise, he did not rise alone, for in his resurrection do we all ascend up into heaven. He fought hand to hand with Death so that Death might not kill us, and he showed us his resurrection so that we might die more willingly because we have hope to live eternally.

Upon those five altars, therefore—of death, burial, resurrection, ascension, and coming of Christ in glory—do we offer up five Thanksgivings, or, rather, five Sacrifices, imitating therein the Phoenix, who makes her own body a burnt offering. The five altars stand prepared before us in order. The Sacrifices are at hand, and they show the extent to which our prayer must resemble the Phoenix, and the extent to which the true and only Phoenix is Christ Jesus.

A Thanksgiving for All Those Benefits
We Reap by the Death of Christ

[Hebrews 2:9–10]

What thanks, O Lord, can we pour forth?
    What hymns shall we sing?
    What praises have we to crown you with?
    Or what gifts worthy enough can we bestow
    upon you, who did not spare your own
    and only dearest Son's blood to save us,
    who were miserable and condemned castaways?
But you, O Lord, in your providence did foresee it,
    that in all your glory and in your wisdom
    and compassion did consent that all
    the health of humankind should consist
    in the death of your blessed Son.
    We were the arch-traitors, but he answered
    all our treasons at a most dreadful trial.
    We had transgressed, but he was the Lamb
    who was to be sacrificed.
Glorified be your name for being so full of pity.
    Glorified be your Son's death
    for being so full of charitable pity.
Let us reckon before you, O Father,
    and between us and our souls how much
    we are indebted for this, your Son's surety.
    We owed all, and he paid the utmost farthing.
    Let us sum up the tally of this account and take note
    of our gains and his losses in this voyage:
    He ventured his life and lost it;
    we ventured nothing but were upon the point
    of shipwreck, and yet we came home survivors.
    By his death we were engrafted into the Tree of Life;

his blood gave it nourishment.
His nailing on the cross cleft the doors of hell asunder
and opened wide the gates of heaven.
Christ, by this means, has become
our Way, our Guide, our Haven.
Would we walk safely? Christ is our path.
Would we not stumble? Christ is our leader.
Would we not be cast away? Christ is our pilot.
What need we now to fear?
Whom should we fly from now?
For Satan's head is broken asunder,
sin is vanquished, Death is overcome,
hell is swallowed up, the Devil who
had power over Death is put to flight.
Before, we lived in slavery, but now we dwell
within the liberties of the Holy City.
Before, we were spotted and foul as lepers,
but the precious drops that fell from Christ's side
have cleansed our souls, and they gleam
as white as snow. In a most desperate state
we lived before, but now in the most happy,
for we are bought and paid for, and no one
can lay claim to us but Jesus Christ.
To repay him for his love (though there is nothing
in us of value that can give him satisfaction)
rather than to pay no part of the debt,
let us recompense as much as we can make—
and that is, not to forget his kindness,
a thing that we should never do.
Let us print him in our hearts,
engrave him on our hands,
write him on our breasts,
yea, wear him in our garments.
Let the sorrows of his suffering
be forever before our eyes.

When we sit down to meat, let us think upon
the traitor who dipped his finger with him
in the dish. When the night approaches,
let it be a memorial of his being apprehended
with billhooks and staves. It was a deed
of darkness and, therefore, done in the night.
When we do but stretch forth our arms,
let us call to mind how he was racked upon the cross.
The branches of these meditations will bear fruit;
by turning over the leaves of his death and passion,
we shall read the story of our own end, and nothing
can more frighten us out of the company of sin
than when we look upon that place to which
we are sure to go—and that is the grave.
So, to meditate is to live well, for no pill remains
to make death taste bitter afterward
unless it were swallowed before.
Those who thus fight are sure to conquer.
Those who conquer are sure to be crowned.
Those who are ambitious of that crown
will desire to be dissolved and to be with Christ.
Those who so desire do not die patiently,
but live patiently and die joyfully.
Such a death, O Lord, let me die,
for in the sepulcher of your Son,
Death, which once was terrible,
is swallowed up, so that now we may
triumphantly sing, "Where is thy sting,
O Death? Where is thy victory, O Hell?"[1]
"The sting of Death is sin," but that is taken out.
"The power of sin is the Law," but that is satisfied.
Thanks, therefore, and immortal honor be given
to our glorious God, who has given us
so noble a victory through the death
only of Jesus Christ. Amen.

A Thanksgiving for All Those Benefits
We Reap by the Burial of Christ

[Psalm 16:9–11]

The grave is full of horror, the house of the dead
    is the habitation of sadness,
      for the body receives no comfort
      when it comes to lodge in this last
      and farthest inn. When our feet
      step upon that shore, we are robbed
      of all our honors, stripped out of all
      our gay attire, despoiled of all our gold
      and silver, forsaken by our friends,
      fled from by our kinfolk, yea, abhorred
      to be looked upon by our own children.
      Nothing is left us but a poor mantle
      of linen to hide our nakedness;
      that is the last apparel we must wear,
      and when that is worn out,
      we must be turned out of all.
A dreadful thing, therefore, would it be to dwell
    in this land of everlasting silence
      and darkness, except that Christ himself
      has gone there before us. How infinitely
      are we bound to him, that in this battle
      of Death, we are not thrust upon
      any danger but what he has gone through.
      How above measure does he love us
      to try the ice first before he lets us venture over?
      He went into the grave before us
      to show that we all must follow him.
      But what riches may we gather
      out of this sepulcher? What treasure

lies hid in these coffins of the dead?
This clear gain we gather, this profitable knowledge we learn:
    that as Adam was made of a piece of clay,
    so all the sons of Adam must crumble
    into dust. The wombs of our mothers
    are the first lodgings that we lie in,
    and the womb of the earth is appointed
    to be the last. The grave is a target
    at which all the arrows of our life are shot,
    and the last arrow of all hits the mark.
Yet, O Lord, let us not repine, whether in the morning,
    at noon, or at midnight—that is to say,
    in our cradle, in our youth, or in our old age—
    we go to take our long sleep. But let us
    make this reckoning of our years,
    that if we can live no longer, that is
    to us our old age, for those who live
    so long as you appointed them
    (though they die in the pride of their beauty)
    die in their old age. Since the worms
    must be our last companions,
    and the pillows upon which we are
    to rest forever are within dead men's skulls,
    what should we be proud of?
Why should we disdain the poorest beggar
    when the hand that sways a scepter
    and the hand that holds a sheep hook
    being found together in the earth
    are both alike? What madness is it
    to pamper the flesh with elegant meats
    and costly wines when (do what we can)
    we do but fatten it for crawling vermin?
    What folly is it to clothe our body
    in sumptuous attires when (let them

be ever so gorgeous) we shall carry
with us but a winding sheet?
We do bathe our limbs in sweet water
and embalm our bodies with rich perfumes
when no carrion in the world can smell
more noxious than must our own carcasses.
Blessed, therefore, be the sepulcher that held
our Savior's body, since it is a book
in which we may learn how to condemn
this foolish love of ourselves.
Happy was your burial, O Jesus, who prepared
our way to our last habitation. Thanks
be rendered to you for your love.
Glory to God, your Father, for his compassion
toward humankind. So be it. Amen.

A Thanksgiving for All Those Benefits
We Reap by the Resurrection of Christ

[*1 Corinthians 15:20-26*]

Christ is risen again. Oh, happy tidings!
    Oh, blessed message! He is risen
    from an ignominious death to a life full of glory.
    He is risen now to fall no more.
    His enemies have done their cruelty;
    Death has done his worst;
    hell has spit forth her venom—
    yet in spite of their malice
    Christ is risen in triumph.
Receive your lights again, you lamps of heaven.
    Darkness, fly from the world.
    You graves that yawned and cast out
    your dead, close up your devouring jaws.
    Since Christ is risen, let all the world rejoice,
    just as, at his crucifying, all the world
    felt pain in his suffering.
How happy are we miserable humans made by this
    resurrection of our glorious Redeemer!
    For now are we sure that our bodies
    fall not like the body of a beast (for then
    our state would be more than wretched),
    but that the Lord kills and makes alive again
    and that he brings down to the grave
    and fetches up again.
My Redeemer now lives, and by his life
    do I know that I shall rise out of the earth
    at the latter day, and that I shall be clothed
    again in my frailty, as my Savior was
    at his resurrection, in his own flesh.

What a blessing, therefore, is by this means
     poured upon us! For although our bodies
     are laid down to rest in deformity,
     in ugliness, in contempt, in baseness,
     in poverty, and in dishonor—yet shall they be raised
     in beauty, in brightness, and in glory.
We were afflicted in Christ when we saw him
     hanging on the cross in torment,
     but we are made joyful in Christ,
     seeing him raised from the dead in triumph.
     The cogitation of this, his resurrection,
     and consequently of our own
     calling up from death to life,
     is a spur to us, while we are on earth,
     to run the race of blessedness.
We are not to awaken out of our dead sleep
     and be appareled with the selfsame flesh,
     skin, and bone for nothing, but there is
     a goal proposed and a garland propounded;
     and to win that, we must begin to run in this life.
Give, therefore, O God, alacrity to our hearts,
     that with cheerfulness we may set forward.
     Give wings to our souls, that with swiftness
     we may make our flight.
     Give strength to us in our race,
     that we faint not till we come to the end.
     And give us grace to run well without stumbling,
     that we may win the prize with honor.
Grant, O Lord, that we may go into our graves
     in peace; so shall we be sure
     to come from our graves in gladness.
     Glorified forever be your name, which works
     these wonders of salvation for us.
     With all admiration, let us adore you,

who holds out such bright crowns
of immortality for us.
Let us, O Lord, deserve them on earth,
to be promised them at our departure from earth,
and to wear them with you in heaven. Amen.

A Thanksgiving for All Those Benefits
We Reap by the Ascension of Christ

[Ephesians 4:7-9]

Lift up your eyes, O you sons of Adam, and behold
    your Savior ascending up into the clouds.
    Bitter was his death;
    his resurrection victorious;
    but his ascension glorious.
    He died like a lamb,
    he rose again like a lion,
    but he ascended like an eagle.
    By his death did he quicken us to life;
    by his resurrection did he raise us to faith;
    by his ascension did he lift us up to glory.
    The resurrection of Christ is our hope,
    but the ascension of Christ is our glorification.
He ascended into heaven—but how?
    He shut not the gates of heaven upon us
    but went there on purpose to make
    the way plain before us. His body is in heaven,
    but his majesty abides upon earth.
    Here he was once according to the flesh,
    and here he is still according to his divinity.
    Absent is Christ from us,
    yet is he still present with us.
    Would you see him?
    Would you touch him?
    Would you embrace him?
    Your eyes have sight too weak
    to pierce through the clouds;
    his brightness is too great and
    would strike you blind with dazzling.

Your hands are too short to reach
up to the seat where he sits;
and your arms not of compass
big enough to be thrown around his body.
But let your faith open her eyes,
for she can behold him.
Let your faith put out her hand,
and with the least finger she can touch him.
As our forefathers held him in the flesh,
so must we hold him in our hearts.
By his ascending up into heaven are we sure
that he is the very Son of God,
for none can ascend there
but he who comes from there.
Celebrate, therefore, this, his ascension, with faith
and with devotion, and you will soon
be in heaven with him. There he sits
at the right hand of his Father,
like an attorney in our behalf,
pleading for mercy; and like a petitioner,
still representing our prayers and complaints
to his heavenly Father.
How happy are we to have such a speaker for us!
How miserable are those if Christ
is not their intercessor!
Then, since our Redeemer has begun
so happy and glorious a voyage,
only to kindle in us an ambition
to follow him, let us, therefore, hoist up
all the sails of duty and obedience, of zeal
and holiness, to arrive in that same haven.
The ladder that must reach up to heaven,
and by which we must climb,
has many steps of righteousness.

The burdens that keep us from ascending
are infinite in number—and they are our sins.
Give us strength, O Lord, to throw them down.
Give us grace to lay hold of the ladder.
The reward of this conquest shall be ours.
The glory shall be yours.
The path that we must tread
to the land of happiness is beaten out
by your Son, but our welcome
must be from your lips.
Say to us, therefore, "Come, you blessed;
    enter the city of the Lord;
    fall down before his throne
    and cry 'Glory, glory, glory,'
    now and to the world's end." Amen.

A Thanksgiving for All Those Benefits
We Are to Receive by Christ's Coming in Glory

[Mark 13:26–27]

Behold, the gates of heaven stand wide open.
    Armies of angels are mustered together,
    the apostles keep their places,
    the evangelists their offices,
    the saints their degrees, and all
    are attendant upon our Lord and Savior,
    Christ Jesus, who sits upon a throne
    of majesty and is coming to judge the world.
At the sight of this, the wicked tremble
    and call for mountains to cover them,
    but the godly rejoice and are proud
    of this high day of triumph.
The goats howl, for they are to be sent to hell:
    "Go, you cursed!"[2] But the lambs skip
    for joy that they shall hear
    a voice cry, "Come, you blessed!"
    Who, therefore, would not put on his
    wedding garment to meet such a bridegroom?
    Who would not put on the armor of faith
    to fight under such a banner?
Upon this day shall we behold him who
    in himself is Alpha and Omega,
    In the world is the Maker and the Maintainer,
    in his angels is their power and their beauty,
    in the church is a father to a family,
    in our souls as a bridegroom to a bride,
    to the just as a bulwark,
    to the reprobate as a battering ram.
What eye has seen, what ear has heard,

what understanding can comprehend
the excellence of this heavenly city?
From there, the king of that city,
so full of majesty, comes in person
and in progression to conduct us there.
There is security without fear,
peace without invasion,
wealth without diminishment,
honors without envy.
There is all blessedness,
all sweetness, all life, all eternity.
There your hunger shall be filled
with the bread of life, your thirst quenched
with the fountain of goodness,
your nakedness clothed
with a garment of immortality.
The comforts we shall receive upon
this blessed day of peace
are that we shall see and behold
our God who has created us,
our Lord Jesus who has redeemed us,
and the Holy Ghost who has sanctified us.
Come, therefore, speedily, O God;
for your elect's sake, hasten
to this great and general session;
and grant, O merciful Father,
that our accounts may be found
so just that we may receive
the rewards of good stewards.
Make us, O Lord, to be Doves in our lives,
innocent and without gall;
to be Eagles in our meditations,
clear-sighted and bold to look upon you;
to be Pelicans in our works,

charitable and religious; and lastly,
to be as the Phoenix in our deaths,
that after we have slept in our graves,
we may rise up in joy with your Son,
and ascend with him up into heaven,
and there at your hands receive
an immortal crown of everlasting glory. Amen.

PART FIVE

Feathers

Short, Pithy Meditations to Accompany

the Prayers in This Book[1]

God is to you all things.
    If you are hungry, God is your bread;
    if you are thirsty, God is your drink;
    if you are in darkness, God is your light;
    if in nakedness, God puts upon you the garment
        of immortality.

—AUGUSTINE

God: the true and only life,
    in whom and from whom and by whom
    all good things are that are good indeed.
God: from whom to turn away from is to fall,
    to whom to turn is to rise again,
    in whom to abide is to dwell forever.
God: from whom to depart is to die,
    to whom to come again is to revive,
    and in whom to lodge is to live.

—AUGUSTINE

Whatever is not of God has no sweetness;
    whatever he gives me, let him take all away,
    as long as he gives me only himself.

—AUGUSTINE

God is Alpha and Omega, beginning and ending.
    In the world, God is the Ruler;
    in angels, their glory;
    in the church, a Father of a family;
    in the soul, as a bridegroom in the bedchamber;
    in the good, a helper and protector;
    in the wicked, a fear and horror.

—AUGUSTINE

If God hears our prayers, he is merciful;
    if he will not hear them, yet he is just.

—AUGUSTINE

God is length, breadth, height, and depth.
    He is length in eternity; breadth in charity;
    height in majesty; depth in wisdom.

—BERNARD

Have you a desire to walk? "I am the way," says Christ.
    Would you not be deceived? "I am the truth."
    Would you not die? "I am the life."

—AUGUSTINE

No one can take Christ from you
    unless you take yourself from him.

—AMBROSE

Christ, our Redeemer, in his birth was a man;
    in his death, a lamb;
    in his resurrection, a lion;
    in his ascension up to heaven, an eagle.

—GREGORY

Christ is honey in the mouth,
    music in the ear,
    and gladness in the heart.

—BERNARD

In Christ's doctrine we find true wisdom;
    in Christ's mercy is found justice;
    in his life is found temperance;
    in his death is found courage.

—BERNARD

Christ is so much the more worthy of honor among us
    by how much he suffered the more dishonor
        in our behalf.

—GREGORY

"O my people, see what I have suffered for you.
　　There is no grief comparable to this of mine on the cross.
　　I who die for you, cry to you:
　　See what punishments I endure;
　　see how I am nailed and how I am pierced.
　　If my outward sorrows be so great,
　　the grief that is within me must needs
　　be greater because I find you unthankful."

—BERNARD

In vain does he wear the name of Christian
　　who is not a follower of Christ.
　　What good is it for you to be taken
　　for that which you are not
　　and to usurp a title that is not your own?
　　If you want to be a Christian,
　　do those things that belong to Christianity
　　and then challenge the name.

—AUGUSTINE

He is a Christian who, even in his own house,
　　acknowledges himself to be a stranger.
　　Our country is above. In that inn, we will not be guests.

—AUGUSTINE

A Christian can take no hurt by being thrown into captivity,
　　for even in his fetters, God comes to him.

—AUGUSTINE

A Christian is not to have confidence so much
    in the beginning as in the ending.

                      —GREGORY

You are a "freshwater" soldier, O you who are a Christian,
    if you hope to overcome without a battle
    or to triumph without a victory.

                      —CHRYSOSTOM

It is not such an honor to be good among those who are
        good,
    but to be good among those who are evil.

                      —GREGORY

A godly conversation overcomes your enemy,
    edifies your neighbor,
    and glorifies your Maker.

                      —ISIDORE

He who waits on Christ must be of such a conduct
    that his outward manners may be
    but glass to show the inward mind.

                      —BERNARD

Such as we are ourselves,
    in such company we delight.

                      —JEROME

Our looks and our eyes cannot put on masks
    tightly enough to hide a bad conscience,
    for the wantonness of the mind is drawn in the face,
    and the actions of the body betray the conditions
        of the soul.

—JEROME

Woe to the heart that is double;
    it gives one half to God and another to the Devil.
    God, being angry that the Devil has a share in it,
    gives away his part too, and so the Devil has all to
        himself.

—AUGUSTINE

In the world, the heart is weighed by the words,
    but with God, our words are weighed by the heart.

—BERNARD

Let not your face and your heart be of two colors.
    Your face looks upward; let not your heart look
        downward.

—BERNARD

The heart has four duties to fulfill:
    What to love, what to fear,
    what to rejoice in, and for what to be sad.

—BERNARD

Among all the creatures that live under the sun,
  there is none that has a heart more excellent
  than that of humans,
  nor more noble, nor more like to God,
  and that is the reason that God asks nothing
  from your hands but from your heart.

—HUGH[2]

The heart is of itself but little,
  yet great things cannot fill it.
  It is not big enough at one meal to satisfy a bird,
  and yet the whole world cannot satisfy it.

—HUGH

The Devil has a will to hurt, but not power,
  because a Greater controls this;
  for if he should do as much hurt
  as he desires to do, there would not be left
  one righteous person living.

—AUGUSTINE

The Devil's service is the worst of all others,
  because he is never pleased with any duty that is done
    for him.

—GREGORY

Where discord dwells, God never comes near the door.

—AUGUSTINE

As God takes delight in nothing so much
    as in love, so the Devil takes pleasure
    in nothing more than the death of love.

—GREGORY

No misery is greater than to leave God for the love of Gold.

—JEROME

What good can a chest full of riches do you
    if you carry around an empty conscience?
    Your desire is to have goods, but not to be good.
    Blush, therefore, at your wealth, for if your house
    be full of goods, it has a master in it who is nothing.
    What profit does a rich man get by that which
    he has if he has not God too, who is the Giver?

—JEROME

The disease of riches is pride.

—JEROME

Riches are not sin,
    but it is sin not to let the poor have a part in them.

—CHRYSOSTOM

Live so that whatever you do may be
    as if it were done in the presence of your enemy.

—SENECA

There is nothing higher than humility,
    which, as if it were always in the superior,
    knows not how to be extolled higher.

                                    —AMBROSE

Our country is aloft; the way to it is below.
    If, then, you would travel upward,
    why do you go out of the path that leads there,
    which is the path of humility?

                                    —AUGUSTINE

Humility is a glorious robe that pride herself
    does desire to put on, lest she should be disdained.

                                    —BERNARD

It is more honor to avoid injury by silence
    than to get the better of it by words.

                                    —GREGORY

If you would be revenged, only hold your tongue,
    and you give your enemy a mortal wound.

                                    —CHRYSOSTOM

He who makes his belly his god makes for himself a new god.
  So many sins as we have, so many gods we have.
  I am angry; anger is then my god.
  I have seen a woman and have lusted after her;
  I make lust my god.
  Whatever we desire and make much of,
  that we make our god.

—JEROME

When we are proud, it is a great misery,
  but when God is humble, it is a great mercy.

—AUGUSTINE

Listing of Prayers by Part Title

PART ONE: THE DOVE

A Prayer for a Child Going to School
A Prayer for a Farmer
A Prayer for an Apprentice Going to Work
A Prayer for the One Who Buys and Sells
A Prayer for a Chambermaid
A Prayer for a Man in Service
A Prayer for a Sailor Going to Sea
A Prayer for Sailors in a Storm at Sea
A Thanksgiving for Sailors' Safe Landing
A Prayer for a Soldier Going into Battle
A Thanksgiving for a Soldier after Victory
A Prayer for a Woman Great with Child
A Prayer for a Midwife
A Thanksgiving after a Woman Delivers Her Child
A Prayer for One Who Is Sick
A Prayer for Those Who Visit the Sick
A Prayer for One in Jail
A Prayer for a Prisoner of War
A Prayer for Those Who Work in Dangerous Places,
    as Coal Pits, Mines, Etc.
A Prayer for One Who Is Poor

PART TWO: THE EAGLE

A Prayer Offered by the Late Queen Elizabeth
A Prayer for the King
A Prayer for the Queen
A Prayer for the Prince of Wales
A Prayer for the Council
A Prayer for the Nobility
A Prayer for the Church
A Prayer for the Clergy
A Prayer for the Judges of the Land
A Prayer for the Court
A Prayer for the City
A Prayer for the Countryside
A Prayer for a Magistrate
A Prayer for a Lawyer
A Prayer for the Universities
A Prayer for the Confusion of Those Who Would Harm Our
    Nation by Violence
A Prayer in Time of Civil War
A Prayer to Withhold the Pestilence
A Prayer in Time of Famine
A Prayer in Time of Persecution
A Prayer for the Head of a Family

PART THREE: THE PELICAN

A Prayer for the Morning
A Prayer against Pride
A Prayer against Envy
A Prayer against Wrath
A Prayer against Sloth
A Prayer against Covetousness
A Prayer against Gluttony

A Prayer against Lust
A Prayer against the Temptations of the Devil
A Prayer for the Evening

PART FOUR: THE PHOENIX

A Thanksgiving for All Those Benefits
   We Reap by the Death of Christ
A Thanksgiving for All Those Benefits
   We Reap by the Burial of Christ
A Thanksgiving for All Those Benefits
   We Reap by the Resurrection of Christ
A Thanksgiving for All Those Benefits
   We Reap by the Ascension of Christ
A Thanksgiving for All Those Benefits
   We Are to Receive by Christ's Coming in Glory

Notes

Notes to the Introduction

1. Ernest Rhys, *Thomas Dekker* (London: Vizetelly, 1887), 36.

2. Algernon Charles Swinburne, *The Age of Shakespeare* (New York: Harper & Brothers, 1908), 104.

3. Ben Jonson and William Drummond, *Notes of Ben Jonson's Conversations with William Drummond of Hawthorndon, January 1619*, ed. David Laing (London: Shakespeare Society, 1842), 4.

4. Dekker collaborated with a team of writers on the play *Sir Thomas More*, and some scholars believe one passage was written by Shakespeare.

5. *Encyclopaedia Britannica*, 11th Edition, Volume 7 (Cambridge: Cambridge University Press, 1910), 939–40.

6. Thomas Dekker and Thomas Middleton, *The Roaring Girl*, Act 3, scene 3.

7. Playwright John Webster, quoted in Marchette Chute, *Shakespeare of London* (New York: Dutton, 1949), 286, Webster was praising "Mr. Shakespeare, Mr. Dekker, and Mr. Heywood"—all three—for their prolific output.

8. R. B. McKerrow in his introduction to Thomas Dekker, *The Gull's Hornbook*, ed. R. B. McKerrow (London: De La More Press, 1904), iii.

9. Nearly 40,000 Londoners died of plague in 1603. Half that many died in the 1608–1609 outbreak. See C. N. Trueman, "London and the Great Plague of 1665," *The History Learning Site*, http://www.historylearningsite.co.uk/stuart-england/london-and-the-great-plague-of-1665/.

10. Mary Leland Hunt, *Thomas Dekker: A Study* (New York: Columbia University Press, 1911), 146.

11. Dekker, *Gull's Hornbook*, 51.

12. Hunt, *Thomas Dekker*, 146.

13. For a discussion of Shakespeare's and other Elizabethan writers' use of the Book of Common Prayer, see Daniel Swift, *Shakespeare's Common Prayers: The Book of Common Prayer and the Elizabethan Age* (Oxford: Oxford University Press, 2012).

14. Swinburne, *Age of Shakespeare*, 105.

15. Hunt, *Thomas Dekker*, 146.

16. Dekker, *Gull's Hornbook*, iii.

17. The phrase was first used in an obscure poem by another Elizabethan poet a few years before Dekker, but Dekker's song "O, The Merry Month of May" from *Shoemaker's Holiday* was where the phrase was first popularized.

18. The poem first appeared in a 1603 play, *Patient Grissel*, co-written by Dekker, Henry Chettle, and William Haughton. The song is sung by the character Janiculo, Act 4, scene 2.

19. For instance, C. S. Lewis, *The Collected Letters of C. S. Lewis, Volume III: Narnia, Cambridge, and Joy 1950–1963* (New York: HarperCollins, 2007), 610; and C. S. Lewis, *Spenser's Images of Life*, ed. Alastair Fowler (Cambridge: Cambridge University Press, 1967), 5.

20. C. S. Lewis, *Studies in Medieval and Renaissance Literature* (Cambridge: Cambridge University Press, 1966), 8–9. The title page of *The Witch of Edmonton* also lists William Rowley and John Ford as coauthors, and some scholars believe John Webster may also have been involved.

21. Thomas Dekker, *Shoemaker's Holiday*, Act 5, scene 4.

Notes to the Prologue

1. (*Editor's Note*: All notes in Dekker's text hereafter are by the editor, not Dekker.] Christian tradition has long identified the pelican as a symbol for Christ. The earliest version of this is found in an anonymous second-century bestiary called the *Physiologus*. Chapter 5 states that a pelican would kill its own young, but then tear open its own side with its beak to revive the chicks with its own blood. Though there is no factual basis for this legend, the pelican became an enduring symbol for Christ, whose blood has salvific power. The symbol is encountered throughout Western literature, being used by Dante, Shakespeare, Gerard Manley Hopkins, and many others.

1. This line that opens Dekker's first prayer is from the 1559 Book of Common Prayer, the fifth collect on days without Communion. Dekker's language is so imbued with words and phrases from the Book of Common Prayer and the Bible that it would be cumbersome to annotate each. Therefore, I have footnoted only those that are directly quoted, are of special interest, or have historical significance.

2. Matthew 19:14

3. Matthew 25:34

4. Revelation 19:1

5. 1 Corinthians 3:6

6. Psalm 104:16

7. This wonderful phrase, "eye service," is from Colossians 3:22 (Geneva Bible): "Servants, be obedient unto them that are your masters according to the flesh, in all things, not with eye service as men pleasers, but in singleness of heart, fearing God." The idea is that servants who perform "eye service" only work hard when the master is looking. As in so many cases, Dekker may well have heard this text read aloud in church, since Colossians 3:15-24 is one of the texts often read as part of the "Solemnization of Matrimony" in the Book of Common Prayer.

8. Probably a reference to Job 8:14: "His confidence shall be destroyed, and his trust shall be a spider's web" (The Great Bible, Coverdale, 1540).

9. Philippians 1:23, Douay-Rheims

10. Romans 6:23

11. Psalm 104:3

12. Matthew 8:25

13. This prayer echoes Dekker's "Prologue, As It Was Pronounced before the Queen's Majesty," which prefaced the first printing of his play *The Shoemaker's Holiday*. In it, Dekker says that he presents the play to Queen Elizabeth with all humility and fear, "as wretches in a storm (expecting day) / With trembling hands and eyes cast up to heaven, / Make prayers the anchor of their conquered hopes" (Prologue, lines 1-3).

14. Isaiah 66:1

15. Matthew 6:9

16. John 5:8

17. Psalm 41:1

18. Most likely Dekker had the famous Battle of Lepanto in mind when he wrote this prayer. It took place around the time he was born

and was one of the last sea battles fought between galleys powered by long-oarsmen. When the Catholic "Holy League" navy triumphed in the engagement, they were able to free as many as twelve thousand Christian "galley slaves" from the Ottoman ships.

19. In these lines there may be a distant echo of Faustus's "Eleventh Hour" speech: "See, see where Christ's blood streams in the firmament! / One drop would save my soul, half a drop." Christopher Marlowe, *Dr. Faustus*, ll. 1432–33.

Notes to Part Two

1. This is, of course, King James I of England, the successor to Elizabeth I and, among other achievements, the royal advocate for the Bible translation that bears his name.

2. Anne of Denmark married James in 1589, when she was fourteen years old. Three of their children survived infancy, including the eldest, Henry, her favorite, and Charles, who later became king upon James's death in 1625. Anne died in 1619. She is thought to have been a Catholic at some time in her life, but she apparently died a confirmed Protestant. The traitors and parasites that Dekker refers to may well be references to her Catholic acquaintances.

3. This reference to Anne's "work" being hidden for a number of years is probably a reference to the gap between the births of her two eldest sons, Henry Frederick, Prince of Wales (1594–1612), and Charles (1600–1649). Between the births of those two, the queen gave birth to two daughters and had one miscarriage.

4. Prince Henry Frederick, Prince of Wales, was the eldest son of James I of England and Anne of Denmark. He was greatly beloved by the people, but his life was cut short when he died of typhoid fever in 1612, a mere three years after Dekker published this prayer for him. Henry was succeeded by his younger brother, Charles, who later went on to have his own problems with civil war, losing his life in 1649 to Cromwell's government.

5. These are biblical measures. "True balaunces, true weyghtes. A true Epha & a true Hin shall ye have. I am the Lord youre God which brought you out of the lande of Egypt" (Leviticus 19:36, The Great Bible, 1540).

6. In this prayer, Dekker has in mind Oxford and Cambridge, the two oldest universities in England. The University of Oxford was founded

sometime in the twelfth century, while the University of Cambridge was established in the following century, in 1209.

7. Much of this prayer refers to the Gunpowder Plot, which had taken place three years earlier. A man named Robert Catesby, along with twelve other conspirators, plotted to blow up Parliament and assassinate King James in one supreme act of terrorism, by igniting thirty-six casks of gunpowder planted beneath the House of Lords. The plot was discovered on November 5, 1605, probably within hours of the time when the fuse to the explosives was to be lit.

Notes to Part Three

1. Genesis 2:21-24
2. Amos 6:8
3. That Luke was a physician is mentioned by Paul in his letter to the Colossians: "Luke the beloved physician greeteth you . . ." (4:14, Geneva Bible). Early legends arose that Luke was also a painter of icons. There is no evidence to support this, but by the Middle Ages, hundreds of icons attributed to Luke were displayed in churches as holy relics. Medieval guilds that protected painters adopted Luke as their patron saint.

Notes to Part Four

1. 1 Corinthians 15:55 is the source for this famous quote, although again, Dekker must have been more familiar with it as part of the Order for the Burial of the Dead from the Book of Common Prayer. In the following lines, which are also part of the Order for the Burial of the Dead, Dekker is also quoting indirectly from 1 Corinthians 15:56: "The sting of death is sin: and the strength of sin is the Law" (Geneva Bible).
2. Here again, although parts of this prayer echo the book of Revelation and Matthew 25, the wording is closer to the prayer provided for the first day of Lent in the Book of Common Prayer.

Notes to Part Five

1. Dekker selected these "Short, Pithy Meditations" from a single massive volume called *Flores doctorum pene omnium, qui tum in theologia,*

tum in philosophia hactenus clauerunt, a thematic collection of quotes from the early church fathers. The compendium is over a thousand pages long and was compiled and edited by Thomas of Ireland, Jacques Stoer, and Rowland Bateman, and first published in 1593. The title used for this section, "Feathers," is not in Dekker's original; it was provided for this edition as a way of continuing the avian theme.

2. It is delightful to see these quotes from St. Hugh, a widely venerated English saint. He was the patron saint of shoemakers, which has special relevance to Dekker, because the hero of Dekker's *Shoemaker's Holiday* frequently invokes St. Hugh.

Bibliography

Brooke, C. R. Tucker, and Nathaniel Burton Paradise. *English Drama, 1580–1642*. Boston: D. C. Heath, 1933.

Cawdrey, Robert. *The First English Dictionary 1604: Robert Cawdrey's A Table Alphabetical*. Oxford: Bodleian Library, 2015.

Chute, Marchette. *Ben Jonson of Westminster*. New York: Dutton, 1953.

———. *Shakespeare of London*. New York: Dutton, 1949.

Dekker, Thomas. *Four Birds of Noah's Ark*. Edited by F. P. Wilson. Oxford: Basil Blackwell, Publisher to the Shakespeare Head Press of Stratford-upon-Avon, 1924.

———. *The Gull's Hornbook*. Edited by R. B. McKerrow. London: De La More Press, 1904.

Hunt, Mary Leland. *Thomas Dekker: A Study*. New York: Columbia University Press, 1911

Jonson, Ben, and William Drummond. *Notes of Ben Jonson's Conversations with William Drummond of Hawthornden, January 1619. Edited with a preface by David Laing*. London: Shakespeare Society, 1842.

Rhys, Ernest. *Thomas Dekker*. London: Vizetelly, 1887.

Shapiro, James. *The Year of Lear: Shakespeare in 1606*. New York: Simon & Schuster, 2015.

Swift, Daniel. *Shakespeare's Common Prayers: The Book of Common*

Prayer and the Elizabethan Age. Oxford: Oxford University Press, 2012.

Swinburne, Algernon Charles. *The Age of Shakespeare*. New York: Harper & Brothers, 1908.

Wells, Stanley. *Shakespeare & Co.: Christopher Marlowe, Thomas Dekker, Ben Jonson, Thomas Middleton, John Fletcher, and the Other Players in His Story*. London: Penguin, 2007.

Acknowledgments

This book would not have found its way into print without the support and hard work of agent Tim Beals of Credo Communications and editor Lil Copan of Eerdmans. Lil's editing of the manuscript was masterly, as was the copy editing of Mary Hietbrink. Tim, Lil, and Mary are clearly the kind of people Thomas Dekker refers to in his introduction to *Shoemaker's Holiday* as "Good Fellows, Professors of the Gentle Craft."

Thank you to Allen Crawford for the exquisite artwork and Kevin van der Leek for the lovely interior design.

I would also like to thank Tim Baker for his excellent proofreading.

Thank you too to Professor Debra Rienstra of Calvin College, an authority on Elizabethan literature, who shared much-needed encouragement and information.